HUSTLE + FLOW = SUCCESS

in Life, Love and Business

Lisa Toste

ISBN-13: 978-1522860549
ISBN-10: 1522860541

Throughout this book, I have made reference to many authors and to information I have learned, discovered, heard, and acquired through my years of study and practice of personal and professional development. To honour each and every one of them, where I do not have a specific webpage or book to cite, I have used an asterisk (*) to illustrate that this is the work of another and I am merely standing on the shoulders of the giants who have gone before me in this field ... and if I have missed anyone, please let me know!

For more information, visit
www.LisaToste.com

Dedication

This book is dedicated to "my "Little Monkeys," Miguel and Sophia Rosa. You are the reason WHY I do what I do!

Remember that everything is possible and you are unlimited in your potential. Create the life of your dreams... everything you need is within you.

I love you!

Testimonials

"The best way I can describe having Lisa Toste as a coach is like going to Disneyland! Absolutely anything is possible... Limiting beliefs need not apply!

It is like working with a Master wizard who truly knows how the laws of the universe work. She shows you exactly what you need to shift or adjust in your own beliefs to get out of your own way! With Lisa there is no glass ceiling so she creates a space that allows you to access parts of your authentic self you never even knew existed. This is _key_ in learning to Manifest your true desires. Since working with Lisa I have successfully quit smoking, drinking, lost weight, quit my corporate job after 20 years and gone on to live my true passion coaching others to do the same. I can truly say I would not be where I am today if it were not for her support as a coach, teacher and mentor.

If you willing to Dream BIG, I highly recommend Lisa Toste, you will not be disappointed!!"

Nicole Gardiner, Life Coach
www.thechangemaker.ca

"Lisa's extraordinary approach to coaching has made my experience with her not only an impactful one but a playful one. Her in depth understanding of masculine and feminine energy is a beautiful blend as she knows exactly how to flow with me and where she can throw a masculine punch to realign me and where to use the feminine caring approach to meet me where I am at the most vulnerable times. Her forte is really coming to understand you and serve you where you are, but to help guide you to where you want to go in an authentic "non-sugar coating" way. The journey with Lisa has been one of true alignment with who I am as we peeled back the layers of life that weighed me down. Thank you Lisa for your unconditional support and professionalism. You truly have a gift!"

Joe Moffett, Author, Speaker, and Performance Coach
www.MasterLifeByDesign.com

"I've been working with Lisa for 2 years now I am incredibly grateful to have her as my coach! I'm pretty sure the sound of her voice contains caffeine due to the fact that through our conversations I always leave energized and in a peak state ready to take on the world! Lisa has guided me and helped me to become the man I am today and as well as taught me how to truly value myself and what I'm capable of! Upon starting with Lisa, writing a book was only my dream and now I am finally publishing my first book! Lisa is loving, empowering, and very strategic with her coaching and is always looking out for your best interests. I wouldn't be where I am today without her and I know I will continue to work with her for years to come!"

Victor Pierantoni, Break Through Strategist
www.Btvictory.com

"Lisa Toste is an OUTSTANDING coach who has facilitated my ability to finally get results by helping me balance out the 2 worlds of: taking action and aligning my energy. In the new world of business and personal success finding the harmony and dance of these two worlds is the completion of a fulfilled person and entrepreneur. I highly recommend her to anyone who is serious about getting results with her wonderful focused, driven yet playful and intuitive energy. She is a delight to work with and is very unique and special gift to the world!!"

Dianne Solano, RNCP, ROHP, Orthomolecular Nutritionist and Health Coach

Contents

Chapter One.
"The Energy-Infused, Action-Plan Martini"

If this book were a cocktail, it would be called "The Energy-Infused, Action-Plan Martini." To create this unique beverage, you would add a measured amount of focused action, a splash of vibrational alignment, a sprinkle of quantum physics, equal amounts of masculine and feminine energy, and a few drops of tequila (the tequila is just to make things a bit fun and unpredictable!). You'd throw it all in the mixer, pour it into a suitably designed glass, and garnish it with gratitude. It would taste strong enough for a man, yet sweet enough for a woman.

Sipping this cocktail, you'd find it somewhat familiar ... like a drink you've always savoured and loved, yet now with a new, updated flavour that tickles your senses as never before.

As the cocktail's effect sets in, you'd come to a heightened state of focus, ready to take massive action. You'd notice that you're suddenly crystal clear on your why and solid in your sense of authentic power and effectiveness.

You'd feel this cocktail giving you courage and the knowledge of how to dance between the masculine and feminine energies within you — your masculine Hustle and your feminine Flow — and you'd intuitively realize that this dance would bring you to a new evolution of mastery, with the power to create results in your life like never before. Connecting deeper to who you are as man or women, but also effectively tapping into another element of yourself, without the fear of coming out of your authentic alignment.

Who would order this drink? Ah ... this is where it gets interesting! This cocktail — this book — is for two different camps of people. It's for BOTH the Hustle (masculine) AND the Flow (feminine) camps!

It's for all you massive action-takers who have found success by DOING. You're my masculine energy people —— **my Hustle people** — living in your yang. I love you, I am you, I work with you, and I coach you. I speak to large audiences of 'you' around the world. You are the men and women who make things happen, forever clamouring ahead (ofttimes like a bull in a china shop) until you do! You are the tribe that values power, strength, individual effort, and bottom-line results, baby!

But ... let's face it ... deep down, you go-getters have a collective nagging concern, don't you? Many of you have realized that there's a mysterious cap on the level of success you're able to achieve through action alone. You've heard lots of talk lately about this powerful, intangible energy force that somehow can help you create even bigger, better, faster results without all that exhausting exertion of forceful effort alone. Behind closed doors, you might even have a sneaking suspicion that there's something real about all this energy stuff, and maybe you're curious enough to explore it a bit. If you identify with this Hustle tribe, keep reading. This book is for you!

Or perhaps, you're in the other group — **my Flow people** — an embracer of feminine energy, fully aware that manifestation occurs through intuition, feelings and staying in the "vortex." You, my dears, are also my tribe. You meditate daily, you can get your body into pretzel-shaped yoga positions, you know how to use energy, Flow, emotion, and the power of the collective conscious. You understand that your thoughts create your reality and that you're not only allowed to expect miracles, but that you witness small miracles on a frequent basis.

Yet ... you've also noticed that things don't seem to manifest as quickly as you'd like or in the ways you prefer. A part of you suspects that if you'd focus more, get more grounded, and take more overt action (dare I say even get a scheduler?), you might actually become more effective.

I feel you. I understand your confusion. This book is for you, my Flow beings!

I intimately know both of these Hustle and Flow camps ... because I *am* both.

I've spent ridiculous amounts of time and energy trying to decode which camp had it right. I was a corporate girl with a background in psychology, an overachiever, logical, and totally jacked up on masculine (Hustle) energy. All I was interested in was results. My masculine drive led me to achieve my career goals, but did nothing whatsoever for my happiness and fulfillment. Showing up for date night with my hubby, me in my corporate, masculine mode of operation, did not create sparks of passion and fun. It actually brought us to the brink of divorce. I had become so comfortable in my masculine energy, I didn't know when it started, or even how to turn it off.

Only when this topic was thrust upon me (more like "forced" actually because I hated this topic initially), did I do a little experiment that forever changed my marriage, my career, my overall happiness, and the power I felt as someone who creates the reality of their life. Of course, since I was still entrenched in my masculine ways of doing things, my initial foray into feminine (Flow) energy had me swinging the pendulum full-throttle into that unknown territory. Being the 'over-achiever' I am, I dove headlong into the world of the collective conscious, manifestation, intuition, and Flow. I had been in these waters before — previously dedicated to my practice of yoga, meditate daily. — *I mean, I spent a month in the Himalayan mountains of Nepal in a Tibet Buddhist Monastery and studied Buddhism.*

I was aware of the power of this energetic space, I just had no idea how to use it or be in it consistently and be in my world of kids, job, husband, traffic, emails, mortgage payments, etc.

For this period of time, while I tried to operate from my Flow exclusively, I set aside my default habits of relying on logic and massive action-taking so that I could experiment with living as much as possible from a space of Flow essence. I was able to reconnect with a mysterious piece of myself; one I had denied for far too long, and I was blown away by how powerful this under-utilized part of me could be —*a part that exists in everyone - regardless of gender.*

While living predominately from my feminine Flow essence was a beautiful and valuable experience, I ultimately realized that it didn't get me the kind of results my goal-oriented personality craved. **What became apparent to me was that living solely from one energy source or the other was dramatically limiting my opportunities, and putting a cap on the results I could achieve.** While my masculine energy had tremendous payoffs, at certain times my feminine energy had tremendous payoffs in other situations.

I found that true success in life only came once I learned to dance between my masculine Hustle and feminine Flow essences. While firmly standing grounded in my core energy.

For a while, I was a horrible dancer. It took me some time to distill all the wisdom and insights I now offer you in this book.

Here is what I have learned from my own life experiences, from study, from my coaching clients, from working with companies large and small, and from speaking to people around the world:

> **"The key to true life mastery lies in the power of harnessing the duality of BOTH your masculine Hustle AND feminine Flow essences."**
>
> *Lisa Toste*

Once you understand the dance of yin and yang, Hustle and Flow, and learn how to use these masculine and feminine energies effectively, you will see incredible results in your individual happiness, , and business success. You will create the life of your dreams. Neither side of this coin alone will get you there. You need to combine the immense power of the collective with your own individual focused action, simultaneously harnessing the *Power of Doing* along with the *Art of Being* in order to create the life you crave and deserve.

You possess both of these different forces within you, whether you're a man, woman, straight, gay or transgender ... all human beings contain the full of spectrum of masculine to feminine energies, regardless of gender or sexual orientation. Different skill sets, actions, and habits typically fall into categories that we, as a society, label as masculine or feminine, but these two seemingly-separate essences actually make up one unified energy source. Once you learn to discern which skill set or energy to tap into for each of your specific desires, bingo! You've discovered the secret sauce, or the secret recipe for creating your own "Energy Infused Action-Plan Martini."

As a speaker and coach I've helped many clients and businesses achieve success by focusing on the Power of Action principle. But as I learned more about the undeniable force of Flow energy qualities, I realized that the Power of Action (masculine energy) was even more powerful when combined with the Art of Being (feminine energy). Not only did they complement and compensate for each other, they actually allowed me to take results or impact to the next level! And that is exciting to me!!!

These two sides of the coin are equal in importance, yet different in the outcome or results each brings to a situation. This is key to understanding that in order to be successful in any area of life, you must know when and how to use each one.

Success to me is defined by the ability to create the feelings, experiences, and events you want to have in life. Success has many different versions to different people. Your definition of success may also change as you hit different phases in life. For example, when I was putting myself through University getting my Psychology Degree, swimming in student payments and debt, I often mentioned I knew I would be successful when I could order a pizza whenever I wanted with whatever I wanted on it. Thankfully my vision for success expanded. It changed again when I entered the corporate world. And changed again when I had babies where merely sleeping for a few hours straight was considered success.

Now as an entrepreneur working with clients from all around the world, from startup companies to established companies with assets in the billions, to people focused on their health, to parents focused on their families, to people working to create impact on the world, and everything in between — *I have noticed a pattern.*

What is interesting to me is that the stuff — the wants and the goals — are always changing. I invite you to expand your version of success to include YOUR ABILITY TO CREATE, to manifest, or to allow the desires in your life to become realized in your experience. This is the skill set that will truly make you successful.

That is what this book will focus on — how to be successful in each moment/situation and with bigger goal setting outcomes.

What is different about this "formula?" Aren't all these results formulas the same? Well, no, they are all not the same. You may have heard of some of the components below before; however, often they are divided on either the Hustle side (define what you want then take action to make it happen) or the Flow side (understand what you want to feel then surrender/allow your energy to attract it into your life). Both concepts are correct — yet one without the other is where the "lack of being successful" in making results happen comes into play. *The Hustle or the Flow formulas are only half the recipe.*

Over time (LOTS OF TIME, I admit) I have come to understand that it's not only the attainment of your end goal that is important (just so we are totally clear, though I still REALLY do like when my clients and I reach the end goals), but it truly is about who you become in the process of the goal coming into manifestation. Initially I was not a fan of the slogan — 'It's not the goal but the journey that is important.' That whole journey thing seemed like a waste of time. Yet, as you go through this book on HOW to be successful in creating, you will start to see not only is it a combination of the dance of Hustle and Flow traits, it is also about the person you become based on this holistic dance that caused you to have your success.

Understanding when to utilize which energy makes all the difference in whether you achieve your desired outcome or totally mess things up. Trust me, I know. I've done both!

Look at the taijitu, the Chinese symbol for Yin and Yang. It looks like two tadpoles forming a circle. One tadpole is white, symbolizing yang (male) energy. The other is black, symbolizing yin (feminine) energy.

Most people think this concept of Yin and Yang is very black and white (pun intended) and there is no middle ground. You're either one or the other. **But within each side there's a circle containing the opposite colour, the opposite energy.** Within the yin space is a dot of yang, and within the yang space is a dot of yin. This symbolizes that each of these seemingly opposite energies contains an element of the other one.

Both Yin and Yang reside within every one of us, but this is not how the majority of us have been raised ... to neither understand nor express ourselves.

Think back to as recently as the 1950's, when men's and women's roles were so clearly delineated in our culture. The ultimate put-down for a male from that generation was to be called "girly" or "sissy," or anything that would remotely imply he embodied feminine energy. A woman would have been equally insulted by any insinuation that she was manly. It's not all that different today, especially in the more patriarchal societies around the world.

Some of us would like to think we're more relaxed in our gender biases. In truth, we've all collected a lifetime of societal clues that cause us to associate certain attributes and ways of being with masculinity, and others with femininity. Even if our intention was to ascribe *no meaning* to these associations, they're so deeply embedded in our collective subconscious that we have very strong conditioning in the matter. We'll be looking more closely throughout this book at what constitutes feminine energy and what constitutes masculine energy.

While each one of us does contain the whole spectrum within us, from masculine to feminine, there is a place on that spectrum where we feel most comfortable. There are certainly exceptions, and this is not related to sexual preference, but the majority of women do naturally feel most comfortable on the feminine side of the spectrum with the majority of men naturally feeling most comfortable toward the masculine end. Yet, being adept at expressing feminine or masculine energy outside of where you feel most comfortable is extremely beneficial.

Today's successful men and women are aware of this, to an extent. A man who identifies primarily with masculine energy gets plenty of messages from the world around him that he should not feel limited to expressing only stereotypical masculine attributes, values, and traits. The 1950's version of a good man does not translate into a successful man of today, and the 1950's guy would definitely be challenged in having a relationship with a modern woman! The ability to take on feminine traits when necessary is a huge asset today for a man who lives primarily from his masculine core, and the reverse can certainly be said for women as well. This book examines this topic more in detail and provides specific strategies.

Problems can arise, however, when we push ourselves to spend the majority of our time expressing an energy that is not aligned with our true, core comfort spot on the spectrum.

It's not uncommon today for women to become stuck predominately in masculine energy, and for men to show up inappropriately feminine in situations where their true masculine power is called for.

This is all done with the best of intentions, and can often have the opposite of a successful outcome if you are not consciously aware of how you are operating in the moment, what the outcome is you want, and if you are not deeply aligned with who you are at your core. I'm going to show you how to dance between your masculine Hustle and feminine Flow essences without losing who you are, most authentically, at your core. I'll guide you through each of the steps of this delicate energy dance, including the final, critical step of coming back home to your authentic power (whether aligned with the masculine or feminine energy).

"The more aware of your intentions and your experiences you become, the more you will be able to connect the two, and the more you will be able to create the experiences of your life consciously. This is the development of mastery. It is the creation of authentic power." Gary Zukav *

I know firsthand how devastating it can be to ignore this all-important step since there was a time when I ignored it myself. Today, I make connecting with my core (feminine Flow essence) a vital necessary and enjoyable part of my daily routine. I no longer worry about getting stuck in my masculine Hustle energy.

Obviously, there are certain attributes, values, talents, and traits that we classify as Hustle or Flow. As we move forward together, I'm going to ask you to stop thinking of these in terms of biological gender. See them instead as simply different parts of us that we all can access any time we choose. As we let go of those gender associations, we discover a new way of playing the game of life — a new way of choosing how we'll interact with people, how we'll create our experiences, how we'll decide which results we want, and how we'll go about manifesting them. This is a major paradigm shift, so I want you to get excited about it!

We're talking about removing barriers and limitations and opening up a whole new way of Flowing with life and others!

And this isn't just a nice, woo-woo idea. Everything in this book is backed up by personal experience, client experiences, and data. I'll be showing you studies that have demonstrated how women in business are more successful when they monitor themselves to ensure they're using both Hustle and Flow qualities (as opposed to focusing on the masculine traits we've come to believe are the keys to business success). Other studies will point out that globally there is a growing demand for feminine values in leadership, in the way businesses are being run and in overall workplace dynamics. Even the traditionally masculine-anchored political and economic structures we've depended on for centuries are starting to shift now — ripe for an energetic overhaul.

The dance between Hustle and Flow, masculine and feminine energies, Yin and Yang, provides the framework for these exciting breakthroughs while honouring the values of both the masculine and the feminine.

I'm going to help you understand the unlimited potential within you as a dynamic energy source of both masculine and feminine frequencies. I'm going to show you how to use this information to get the success you want, create the impact that inspires you, and experience the life you desire. Believe me when I tell you that knowing and applying this information in your life will be nothing less than transformative. I say this from personal experience as well as from witnessing the changes in the many clients I have coached in this arena.

This is not information we learned in school or from our parents. Social structures based on the old paradigms we grew up with are breaking down fast. Relationship roles, office dynamics, parenting practices ... the traditional rules we learned for conducting ourselves in each of these areas no longer fit in such a black and white way! And in our attempt to adjust to the new ways of our time, we've received lots of mixed messages and crossed signals about it. This information about feminine and masculine energies will help to sort it out for you, will free you, and open up a whole new vista of possibilities for you as it has for me.

Imagine how amazing it will be to finally have a system for knowing how to best show up for all the various situations in your life!

Imagine how good it will feel to be able to dance between each of your energetic frequencies and dial up the potency of your authentic, powerful self!

Up until now, it's likely your goal strategies have been either strictly masculine in their approach (focused on an action plan) or strictly feminine (centered on the feeling and energy plan). Both strategies are excellent, yet each of them alone contains only half the groceries you need to make the recipe of your desires.

By the time you finish this book, you'll have pulled together a truly aligned and holistic formula for goal setting and achieving your best results for success. By combining the *Power of Doing* and the *Art of Being*, you're about to ignite the formula I used to transform my own life and the lives of my clients into masterpieces of successful results, dynamic relationships, and an evolution in your personal growth. You will master a way of interacting with yourself and others in the world which is life changing, as well as a paradigm shift in consciousness.

So ... buckle up and enjoy the ride ahead, for truly life will never be the same again! ;)

Are you Naturally More Hustle or Flow?

Are you curious to see how you tend to show up — more Masculine Hustle energy or more Feminine Flow energy in life? It could be different based on situations or you could see you have a standard way to approach life. Neither one is good or bad — simply use this exercise to note where you are.

If your life is exactly where you want it to be in areas of relationships, business, and overall, then keep doing what you are doing. If not (and this is most likely why you picked up this book), then use this as opportunity to notice which side you under-use.

And keep reading this book as we discuss why you may be predominately using this side, and how to increase your desired results by allowing the other core energy to assist you in becoming more successful with achieving your goals and interacting with people!

Hustle or Flow Quiz*

When working on a task which best describes you:

You often get distracted, and may stop and start a few times before the end task is completed. This doesn't really bother you. You have a lot on the go so you tend to do a few things at once. *(Flow)*

... or ...

You get hyper focused on one singular task. It REALLY upsets you when you are distracted or taken off your set course. You start something and drive until it is finished. *(Hustle)*

~~~~~~~

A close family member calls you ... they have a problem and want to talk, do you:

Listen, empathize and help them consider options, the impacts and talk it out? *(Flow)*

... or ...

Focus the conversation on fixing the problem — keeping the conversation short and focused on a solution? *(Hustle)*

~~~~~~~

When having to make a tough decision that may negatively impact people, do you:

Logically look at the 'reality' of the situation? You talk with other people to seek solutions on how to solve the problem, not to gain approval. And, in the end you trust your own ability to make the decision and take necessary steps that must be taken. *(Hustle)*

... or ...

Feel for the individuals impacted? With passion, you look for alternative solutions that can benefit everyone, even if that is not the best outcome for you. You look for inner guidance on the next right action. *(Flow)*

~~~~~~~

As you end your day, do you:

Outline the tasks for tomorrow that align with your goals and schedule them? Prepare mentally and physically for the next day so you can start it off focused and get the best results? *(Hustle)*

... or ...

End the day with a bath or some form of self-care, meditate, journal, or do a gratitude list? Trusting and knowing that you will attract tomorrow what is needed to have your goals unfold as they are meant to. *(Flow)*

~~~~~~~

You have had a challenging day at work. You finally make it home and your partner is there. Do you:

Tell your partner you need to talk and then UNLEASH all the emotions, experiences, and things that happened during the day in a long conversation? When you finish this long rant you feel relief! *(Flow)*

... or ...

You tell your partner in a brief conversation how you overcame the challenges at work and what you accomplished? You then tune out watching TV or on the computer. *(Hustle)*

~~~~~~~

It is date night with your mate. When they asked you where you want to go for dinner, do you:

Feel intuitively where you might want to go, what you want to eat, and what type of atmosphere you want to be in to match your mood? *(Flow)*

... or ...

Come up with one suggestion quickly? No need for a discussion on it. *(Hustle)*

~~~~~~~

When it comes to your goals, do you:

You know what you want, when you want it, and are you ready to take action to get there? It is aligned with your mission and you have tasks organized in your scheduler. *(Hustle)*

... or ...

Know your reasons WHY you want something with better clarity then the actual detail of WHAT you want? You are motivated by the overall impact of a goal, how it will make you feel and/or how this goal will help meet the needs of people. You have much emotion around your goals which provide for a strong drive to make them happen. You often experience little synchronicities along the way to getting your goals. *(Flow)*

~~~~~~~

As a Leader you notice you more inclined to:

Take control, make quick decisions that impact the now, set a course, and follow it to the end? The team is meant to follow you as their leader. There is a chain of command to be respected. *(Hustle)*

... or ...

Collaborate for the team, listen and understand all options and impacts to a decision before making one? When you do decide, you often check for feedback or measure how the plan is working and make changes if needed. Leadership is more heart centred, for the good of the group. *(Flow)*

~~~~~~~

Communication is used to:

Solve a problem or get a result. *(Hustle)*

... or ...

Connect, express emotion or relief stress by talking about problem. *(Flow)*

~~~~~~~

Success is created by:

Taking action and hard work by the individual. *(Hustle)*

... or ...

Aligning your energy and following the next intuitively inspired action. *(Flow)*

~~~~~~~

So, how do you most naturally show up — Hustle or Flow?

The result may or may not have surprised you, but hang on to that information as we move forward because it's time to challenge the rules.

Chapter Two.
Time to Change the Rules of the Game

Before we really dive into the topic of Hustle and Flow — we need to explore and change a few rules —— and introduce some new ones!

Have you ever been in the mirror room of a fun house? You know the room where they have all the mirrors that take your image and make you look different depending on which mirror you look at. There is the mirror that makes you look really tall and skinny (that one is fun), the other one may cause you to look shorter and thicker (yes, that one is not as fun), and others can completely distort your image and make you not even look like you anymore!

Well, those mirrors are similar to our beliefs, expectations, and the mental rules we have about "how things are supposed to be." ***Depending on what mirror you look at — or what mindset you use — you get a different view of the situation.***

So I would like you to suspend your usual judgment, expectations, and rules when it comes to the issue of Masculine and Feminine — Hustle and Flow — while you read this book. You know what I am talking about, right? The standard stereotype that says men must act masculine and women must act feminine — all of the time. THE END —

no adjusting the radio dial. Any deviation from this stereotype is to be judged, shamed, or labeled — like the term 'masculine women' or "feminine man" for example.

At the time of me writing this, I "googled" the term 'masculine women' and got 40,800,000 hits!!! So it tells you there is a discussion going on about whether women are acting too masculine or not feminine enough! Similarly, there is a discussion going on at the other side of the coin asking where all the "Real Men" have gone.

We will go into all that in this book — but here is the key distinction — we need to see this issue via a new mirror because the one we are looking at is faulty and providing disastrous results. Divorce rates are gloomy, poor communication, and passion fizzling away are the top causes of divorce; women are unsatisfied and leaving the traditional workforce; and we are setting up some unhealthy role modeling for the next generations.

What does all of this have in common? We need to change our views on masculine, feminine, and our lack of ability to successfully work with the true dynamics of it. And we need to do this now in order to create our versions of success.

So for now let's play a new game called "The Energy of Hustle and Flow."

The rules for this new game are noted below. We will then dive into some information — but this time you will be able to see it from a new perspective, get new 'ahas' and see how this can directly translate into changing your life, your business, your relationships, how you parent and how you overall YOU!

And the end of the game you can keep what resonates with you, through back what does not — but at a minimum you will be able to say you have CHOSEN your rules, beliefs and patterns in this subject area — and not simply replicated an outdated model of how gender shows up. Because well ... let's be honest, that model is just not working!

New Rule #1: This is Not a Pink or Blue Topic

Are you ready for this twist? Take off your gender glasses and I invite you to see this topic without attributing masculine energy to men and feminine energy to women. That is a bit of a brain scramble right? Now I know a few red flags have just gone up for some people reading this book ... but stay with me here for a moment.

By defining these two energy components of ourselves, which are opposites and complimentary, via gender we have cut half of ourselves off from some key attributes, behaviours and ways of being that are critical for taking your life, experiences and results to the highest form you can.

Now, I am not saying women should start acting more like men and men should become more like women. Again, I am not talking about gender stereotypes here. Not at all ... as you will read in this book, I am suggesting that we deeply and intentionally connect to our core authentic energy on a daily basis. For most women that are feminine and most men that are masculine, we learn the ability to strategically and profoundly tap into our complimentary core energy when needed. So for example, a woman would typically not live in her masculine energy. She would become even more powerful in her feminine energy, lead and live from this space, but also enhance her overall energy by accessing when needed the masculine attributes — like focusing, taking action, making decision, etc., when it serves her. Similarly, for a man, he would typically not live from a feminine space. He would consciously root even deeper to his identity as masculine energy, and in addition be able to improve his leadership and relationships by access his intuition, his listening skills and his ability to focus on relationships.

The ability to see this overall topic as energy — not defined by gender — allows new possibilities and takes away limitations that really are only societal!

Now, don't worry, we will take this out of the intellectual realm and talk real situations and real strategies very soon.

I remember the first time I heard the concept of masculine and feminine energy ... it did not sit so great for me (and that is an understatement) because I saw this topic defined by gender.

Let me share the story ...

This is an example of how my EPIC fail of managing my energies actually lead to my biggest AHA moment. It is also the basis for me highlighting rule#1.

I was interviewing for my ultimate dream job as a life/business coach at one of the top international coaching companies. It was a job I had wanted when I was 23 years old but never applied for, until that is, I found myself in the interview process when I was 40 (this happened through the most amazing turn of events I highlight in the chapter on goal setting).

While applying for my dream job — I received some "interesting" and unexpected feedback from the panel. They mentioned my strengths and aspects that would make me a great fit for the job ... and then they commented about me "living in my masculine energy a bit too much." So kind of like I was a really powerful woman, but 'powerful' more like a bull in a china shop that was wearing really good heels and a nice dress. (Okay, I am paraphrasing, but that was the essence of what they were saying.)

Just 'kind of' powerful because I was operating almost exclusively from my masculine side. I was fresh from spending many years in the corporate world. I often lead multi-million dollar projects, with teams of people (90% being male) and had tough decisions, tight time lines and lots of moving parts and actions to control. So yes … it definitely had an impact over time on how I showed up since so much of my time was spent at work.

At the time, when I got this feedback it took everything in me not to roll my eyes. I managed to maintain my composure and instead, I just looked confused and asked a few key questions that you might also be thinking such as, what the heck does that even mean? And how would I even go about doing that — operating more from my feminine especially in business?

The description I understood of this topic did not sit well with me and seemed more related to gender … sort of like women are feminine and should behave as such and men are masculine. The End. I couldn't see how I could always be feminine and run a business, help others run their businesses, or even run my own household.

I had scored some pretty sweet successes in my life and was more than just a little concerned about changing the whole game plan.

I also knew I was not at my happiest in other areas of my life. My once passionate relationship had fizzled, and I felt a lack of connection with the woman I used to be.

As disturbing as it was in the moment, there really was a gift to this feedback as it caused me to turn off the autopilot switch and start asking myself the right types of questions. I finally took my fingers out of my ears and started to dive into this topic. I just needed to test it myself and see the results.

After much research, personal experiments and experiences, coaching my clients and even speaking to other companies on this topic around the globe during my coaching travels (ooh yeah, you're reading this right! Companies are embracing this information in the workplace.), I have come to understand three key distinctions on the topic of masculine and feminine energy.

This is Not 'Boys vs. Girls'

One key distinction we must make before we start this conversation is to let go of the idea that this topic is a 'boys vs. girls' type of battle of the sexes discussion. This is not a pink or blue concept. This is where the change in perception starts.

Every one of us possesses both Hustle and Flow energies within us, regardless of gender or sexual orientation.

Consider masculine and feminine energy to be on different sides of the same coin. If we can detach these concepts from human physiology, we recognize that each of these energies represents a particular grouping of values, traits and behaviours.

Although it is true that a large majority of women are mostly feminine at their core, this doesn't mean they can't have access to the vast repertoire of masculine energy attributes. The same goes for men who also mainly associate with masculine energy at their core. They, of course, have access to feminine energy as well. The key point here is that regardless of your gender or whether you're more aligned with masculine or feminine energy, and this includes all of their traits, values and behaviours most of the time, you can (and I will go so far as to say you should) access the other energy in order to help you create your versions of success!

The key is to know when and how long to stay in the opposite energy so you don't get stuck there!

Trust me. I know all about getting stuck and we will dive deeper into that discussion in the chapter on misalignment of energies.

In order to make real change, we need to interrupt your pattern of thinking on this topic to view this information with a new pair of glasses. This will allow you to see new possibilities, create new results and live new realities.

The strategy is to know when to use each energy based on the situation, and your needs and/or the needs of the individual you are interacting with.

I want to make sure the point is clear that separateness — — an either/or scenario (you are either masculine energy or feminine energy), is not what I'm supporting here.

When you have that dynamic of separateness, it creates a hierarchy — one being better than the other or opposed to the other.

For example, what is more often seen in our culture is the idea that femininity is weaker, less powerful and not as important as masculinity. Any type of separateness thinking sets up a dynamic for conflict. One is not better than the other. And that is a disadvantage for both men and women. As many men increase their success in relationship and business when they do incorporate feminine labeled qualities such as — listening, connection, being relationship focused, intuition, going inward for internal guidance, just to name a few.

This book focuses on the power of the holistic approach, the power of embracing both energies independent within you.

What is most damaging about this duality type of thinking is that it can lead to shaming. For instance, if masculine energy is only for men and feminine energy is only for women, this creates an environment of ridicule when people step into the other energy space. This is often seen if a woman becomes goal oriented, takes action and becomes outwardly focused. They are deemed wrong for being masculine, with the current trending name being 'masculine women' as in our earlier example.

Similarly, a man can be shamed for being intuitive, in touch with his feelings, or someone who into meditation or his inner guidance. He can be ridiculed for not being seen as a 'real man' who would be more focused on the logical, analytical and more physical version of the world.

In reality, for a woman to be successful in the corporate or business world, masculine energy — or Hustle — provides many advantages, as we will discuss. And if men want to be successful in relationships and as leaders, they gain advantage being able to utilize their feminine energy.

The goal is to know WHEN and how long to stay in these energy spaces. What can be accomplished when you embrace both energies is far more powerful than what you can accomplish with just the use of one.

Consider how the most amazing creation, life itself, is conceived. It requires both aspects of masculine and feminine. How to master that dance is the core concept of this book.

Hustle and Flow: A New Language to Break the Gender Pattern of Thinking

My husband is ex-military and a black belt in martial arts. Any time I have talked about this 'masculine and feminine stuff,' he is all with me ... until I start talking about *him* and *his* feminine energy. He glazes over and I can almost hear his internal dialogue go something like, "there is no way in hell I am embracing my feminine energy."

Now, what is funny is he, like many men, understands and aligns with the talk of intuition, emotion, and the power of collaboration, but since these things are deemed "feminine," it limits their ability to connect with this topic — and this is very much to their disadvantage in creating success in all areas of life.

Similarly, with female clients I coach who want to start their own business for example, focus, get a plan together, and making tough decisions; they fear their relationship being impacted by this type of masculine type energy.

I get it ... but this fear is based on the assumption you need to live in this masculine space all the time.

If we saw this 'masculine' energy and labeled it HUSTLE — the energy of DOING and making things happen via individual effort, then it is not so daunting. It makes sense to show up this way for your business meetings, during power trips to the grocery store (you know what I mean here), or generally trying to get things in order in your life and not so much on date night, right? This is the power of language!

It is similar for a man. I coach many very masculine men with regard to using their focused vibration, energy, intuition, the fuel of their emotions, and being able to be relationship-focused in their businesses and in life. Now, they don't tell many other people they are being coached on this and if I labeled this as 'feminine' energy, I would expect many men would be incredibly uncomfortable.

If not for the amazing results they get when they combine this work with their masculine, I would assume many would stop working with me on these areas.

When I call it FLOW energy — getting into the Flow — working to manifest, align your vibration, focus on the needs of others to foster stronger client, employee and personal relationships well ... that just makes sense and quickly translates into results that pay off!

Throughout this book we will interchange the term Masculine energy with HUSTLE energy and the term Feminine energy with FLOW energy to break the pattern of gender association, which may limit you playing full-out in these areas.

As the book title says this book is going to talk about using both your Hustle plus Flow to create your success!

Living In Your Core Energy

This book is about living in your core energy and strategically knowing when to use the complimentary energy. To be 100% clear, I am NOT suggesting we become 50% masculine (Hustle) and 50% feminine (Flow).

This book will highlight strategies for mastery of knowing when, how, and why to move into each energy to create the impact and outcome you are looking for ... so this is not about a 50/50 draw. *It is about becoming 100% you — and using all the energy you have access to.*

Later in this book, we dive into the topic of energetic alignment. Notice the language here — we are not taking about 'balance.' I don't really understand why we use that word because if we look deeper we are not looking to get an equal amount of work and life outside of work.

I work with many professionals and business owners and this "work life balance thing" is a constant topic that comes up for both men and women. I refer to it more as a "shuffle" rather than balance.

There are times you want to spend more in your Flow state (starting a project that needs creativity, collaborating, nurturing family, listening to a friend going to a hard time, connecting spiritually for guidance, etc.) and there are times when it is GO TIME — and you need Hustle to make quick decisions, get a plan together, and hyper focus on something to get it to completion.

So the dancing with and between Hustle and Flow is key.

Where many concerns come up are in questions such as, "will I, as a feminine woman for example, get "stuck" acting too masculine and have it impact my personal relationship because I am so focused on achieving?" Well, yes that can happen. How do I know — because I was kind of the poster child for that epic error. However, at the 11th hour of almost getting a divorce, I learned how to reconnect back with my feminine in a powerful way.

Connecting With Your Core Energy

You need to consciously and intentionally connect with your core, daily rituals to anchor to your authentic core (mostly feminine Flow for women and masculine Hustle for men), to avoid getting stuck.

It is about becoming more powerful as a Woman who owns her Feminine powers and is able, when needed, to use her

Hustle to make her essence even more focused, powerful, and translated into results.

It is also about a Man deeply rooted in his Masculine nature who also has the flexibility to tap into his emotions, intuition, and essence of his Flow to enhance his relationships and his leadership. He will use his ability to take action resulting in the greater good of everyone.

The Key of this book is to become the most powerful version of a man and dynamic version of a female.

The thing is, that definition may undergo an upgrade ...

Various Schools of Thought

This is not some new age woo-woo topic, although, confession time again ... initially this topic seemed a bit, well, 'out there,' for me. From the content I had read, it either seemed highly academic or too woo-woo. Don't get me wrong. I do appreciate the woo-woo stuff. I just did not understand how I translated this into creating change or results in my life.

I started to do some research and let me tell you, this concept is very well-rooted in both historical and modern data:

- **In Jungian psychology**, one focus centres around the anima and animus, a very complex theory of the unconscious mind. The concept outlines that within a man there is an inner aspect of femininity; and within a female there is an inner aspect of masculinity.*

- **In Eastern cultures** and in different forms of yoga such as Kundalini, you can see the strong focus on both the "twin energies" of masculine and feminine.*

- **In Chinese medicine** and the book of I Ching, the concept of Yin and Yang are core to the diagnosis of ailments and recipes for how to live life. It stresses upon the harmonious balance of the Yin (feminine energy) and Yang (masculine energy). When one of these energies exceeds the other, sickness or dysfunction in life starts to occur.*

All of these schools of thought have a core element of the necessary element of an interdependence of the energies within a person. It truly was amazing for me to discover this because in the Western world, we have very much invoked a rigid duality of the sexes and connected that to the energies. This has caused more harm than good. Now we are at a choosing point where we can decide what is true for us and how we live our lives.

Okay so now you have the new rules for playing the game of Hustle and Flow for success. There are a few twists in here for you to consider I know, but as my favourite quote from Einstein, "We cannot solve our problems with the same level of thinking that created them."*

So, in order to remove limits that are holding us back from creating our successes — we need a new way of thinking.

Chapter Three.
Overriding Myths and Stereotypes

Many of our ideas about masculine and feminine are deemed from stereotypes, media, and marketing. Unfortunately, these outlets do a poor job at truly articulating the power of each energy. Once you can see the importance of each energy, you will get a deeper respect for both your core energy and how to meet the needs and/or utilize the opposite energy. It will become clear how and why you need both your Hustle and Flow to become successful.

For women who are feminine at their core (Flow energy), this chapter is intended for you to really comprehend and take back the power of your femininity. Is it really a wonder so many women have taken to embody masculine energy when the media and many social structures, business world are setup to give messages that femininity is weak/less than ...

It is my intention to highlight the true strength of Flow energy for both men and women to use.

When women can see the amazing combination of deeply operating from your Flow energy and, when needed, sprinkle some masculine energy to help increase your ability to create results amazing transformations start to take place ...

We will go into strategies, habits for women to utilize, and anchor deeper to your Flow energy in a later chapter. For now, the first step is to over-ride some myths and stereotypes about femininity with new information regarding the true reality that the Flow energy holds for anyone who uses it — both men and women.

"Happiness is not a matter of intensity but of balance, order, rhythm and harmony." Thomas Merton*

Men will also be able to see the how deepening into their core Hustle energy serves them, the limits and impacts it has on their relationships, and to create the highest level of results when they cut over their Flow energy.

On the flip side of the coin — using too much or being limited to only one energy can have its down side.

For both men and women (regardless of whether you are gay or straight), understanding the traits of Hustle/Flow energy will help you better understand your mate. At work it is also invaluable to understand different needs and how people will show up based on their core Flow.

As you go through this chapter look for the following information and we will use it in the following chapters:

- What energy do I see myself showing up as most of the time?

- What positive impact does this energy provide to me in my life?

- How often do I use the other energy? Never / Sometimes / Whenever needed?

- What is the impact in my life of me not learning how to dance between the two energies?

Values, Traits and Behaviours for the Energies

Now we are about to outline the values, traits, and behaviours of masculine and feminine energy. The purpose of doing so is for you to see where you may have limiting beliefs surrounding a specific energy, or identify where you maybe be tapping into a particular energy too often or too little. Are you listening to 103 FLOW FM — all feminine energy all day, every day? Or possibly 99.5 THE ROCK — masculine energy with absolutely NO commercial breaks for anything remotely feminine?

Let's first discuss these two aspects. The following chapters will help you learn how to use them in your life.

What is the Definition of Masculine Energy?

Admirable qualities of masculine energy display the ability to quickly get to the point in a conversation, to make a decision, or to take action. The strength of the masculine comes in its ability and determined drive to move forward. When out of balance, it may do so at any cost to achieve the end goal. Masculine energy possesses a logical, systematic, and direct approach to finding solutions.

This energy is more outwardly focused and holds as a priority, the rights, freedoms, and rewards of the individual more so then the concern of the overall group.

The masculine will help you to take control of your life, focus on what needs to be done, and take actions that are necessary to make it happen NOW! The masculine can focus on a singular item until it is completed or resolved without allowing for distractions to take it off course of the goal.

SO, this would be the opposite of multi-tasking. You may have heard the saying if you want to understand a feminine mind, it is like having 3,548 browsers open at the same time on your computer. Well Masculine energy would be the equivalent of having one browser open ... doing the job they meant to do, and not even being tempted to check his Facebook page while doing it.

Masculine — The Energy of DOING

Here are a few words that help understand the traits of Hustle Energy:

- action oriented, mission, and time focused

- brain-centred thinking

- seeks to complete an activity/task

- logical, steady, systematic, consistent

- seeks to protect, defend others

- hierarchical and impatient

- seeks freedom and to fix

- views communication as a form to fix things, arrive at solutions and achieve results

- seeks to reduce — including in language

- controlling and outward-focused

So many women have tried to align with this masculine form of behaviour to be successful in a very "masculine-dominated" business world. And hey, no judgment from me on this. I was the poster child for trying to fit in. I mean, the whole fashion of shoulder pads in women's suit jackets and blouses (if you are old enough to remember that horrible trend), was about being more masculine.

Women being able to tap into the behaviours and traits of masculine energy is undeniable in the world of business; however, as we will discuss more in a later chapter.

Operating from this masculine space predominately puts a woman at a serious disadvantage in many ways, both personally and professionally. I, however, completely get that many women did the smart thing of modeling after success. The problem was that "successful models" in the business world were all men.

So we tried the whole act like a man thing — and, well, it does not work.

And acting 100% from Flow space all of the time in business also does not work (I tried them both personally and still watch many of my clients try this).

Since neither of these approaches work, it is time for a new updated and united approach.

The new economy and business sector require both Hustle AND Flow.

Masculinity Out of Alignment

The masculine energy force is necessary to create results and experiences in your life whether you are female or male; however, an excess or a lack of masculine energy can create outcomes of negative consequences.

To give you an idea **when masculinity is out of balance in a man (too much or too little)**, you may feel a lack of security or the need to keep your guard up when you are around him. It is the opposite of the protective and safe feeling a man rooted in his authentic masculine state will emit in his presence. This lack of balance in masculinity also creates the experience of aggression, hyper-competition, lack of concern for other, lack of feelings or emotion, and selfishness. These can recreate serious difficulties in relationships.

When masculinity is not present enough in a woman, she can feel out of control in her life, overwhelmed, not able to take the actions needed to get the results she wants to create, and can be challenged to focus on the end goal until it is completed. She may also be unable to make a decision or take such a significant time doing so that it has a negative impact on her opportunities and many missed, changed, or lack of timely actions may result in a decision that was made after too much time had elapsed. If masculine energy is too high, she can become less nurturing, cut off from her feelings and her intuition, further viewed as cold, lacking passion, and sex appeal to her partner.*

What is the Definition of Flow Energy?

The powerful force of FLOW has endured both the wrath of being feared for its power or, contrary to this, deemed less important and viewed as weak. However, when feminine energy is viewed outside the context of gender, both men and women can see the power of the divine feminine.

The traits and behaviours of feminine energy are attributed toward introspection, connection to intuition, communication, relationships, and to the greater good of the groups.

This contrasts with what we discussed in the masculine which is focused outwardly, on the greater good of the individual and based more on logic than intuition. The feminine focuses on expanded consciousness and is full of feelings, emotions, and thoughts.

The feminine is in constant movement; it is about change, where masculine will provide stability and at times, rigidness.

By reading these contrasting traits you understand now why the combination of both is so dynamic.

Feminine energy is an explosive type of powerful full energy — and when sprinkling a bit of HUSTLE, you can focus that energy in the right direction to get you the results and create the impact you are looking for.

When it comes to creating results, the masculine will seek to gain a clear singular focus, outline timely activities, and drive on until completion is achieved on deadline, and will not go off course or be distracted.

This, at times, is what is needed both in our personal and professional lives. Nevertheless, if only the masculine is used, there can be a neglect to consider the impact of an action or decision for the team, the end user, or the partner in the relationship. This is where Flow energy is important to offer an alternative perspective to consider.

How the needs of others are meet is not the primary focus of the masculine energy; it is of the feminine. This energy will focus on what the overall impact is to be created for the greater good of the group, and what the end goal feeling is.

The feminine will create a plan, although it can change and will run its course as long as it doesn't negatively impact others. All consequences of a decision will be considered before coming to a final conclusion.

This idea is highlighted by in the following quote by Brigadier General Rachel Weisel of the Israeli army as she discussed how feminine perspective is valued in the Israeli army.

"You know that if a woman participates in a (difficult) decision like going to war" she added, *"all of the implications are going to be considered." p. 80, Althea Doctrine**

You can see how this is a benefit to create harmonious family units, relationships, economies, to run businesses, and in leadership overall. Yet if only the feminine is utilized, then the cost of the individual can be overlooked.

It may be a very long process before any action can be taken and at times, this can have negative consequences.

Not everyone around the dinner table or stakeholder table needs to be on board before a decision is made and action taken.

Feminine — The Energy of BEING

Here are a few words that help understand the traits of Flow Energy:

- focused on being, spontaneous, fluid

- heart-centred, emotional, feeling

- seeks connection and nurturing

- focused on people/ emotions

- intuitive, inward-focused, change

- energetic, soft and radiant

- focused on needs of others and relationships

- not hierarchical and patient

- uses communication to connect, express feelings, and release stress

Feminine Energy out of Alignment

When Feminine Flow energy is out of alignment meaning it can hamper your experiences and ability to create success. Too much Flow energy can cause you to drift — without time and focus to taking necessary actions. It can leave you feeling overwhelmed, out of control in your life and a victim to life circumstances — because you may not feel the power to create your own.*

BUT Flow energy truly is extremely powerful when it can direct is energy to manifesting and aligning vibrations. More on this in the last few chapters.

Five Key Distinctions Between Hustle And Flow

When working with people on this topic, I like to highlight five key distinctions between the HUSTLE and the FLOW. This helps you to see the contrast and critical importance of tapping into energies and their individual possibilities.

These are not in order of importance because personally, I think each one is a powerful distinction on its own. While reading these, think of where you tend to show up more.

What would happen if you injected a bit more of the masculine or feminine approach in your life? Hmmm ... things could get exciting!

Distinction #1: Individual vs. Collective/Group Focus

The first distinction made between masculine and feminine energy, Hustle and Flow, is that feminine energy is more focused on the collective — what's best for the group or team as a whole. In contrast, masculine energy is more focused on the individual. Knowing this key difference will help you understand the many ways each of these energies shows up in different situations, whether personal or work-related. The results we desire and the ways we go about creating those results are impacted largely from which energy we operate primarily.

When you're operating from masculine energy, you're focused on the power of the individual. You have the ability to concentrate on a singular activity for long periods of time in order to achieve a very clear and defined goal.

Consider prehistoric humans. Let's view masculinity via the cavemen hunters who would go out for days on end with the singular goal of bringing back food. They had to learn to focus on this without distraction to ensure the survival of the family. Their individual success determined whether or not their loved ones went hungry.

A typical feminine decision-making thought process involves connecting several different factors and weighing the impact of each. Since the safety and the good of the collective group are important to the feminine, any decision involves careful consideration of multiple options and multiple potential outcomes.

It is not uncommon for feminine-oriented people to put others welfare above their own, which is evident in the typical example of today's burned-out 'supermom.' Getting up every two to three hours for months on end to nurse a baby is a prime example of the feminine tendency to put others' needs before the needs of self. Been there, done that, got the t-shirt!

Consequently, feminine-energy-oriented leaders are going to have a different leadership style from male-energy-oriented leaders. Masculine leaders are likely to compartmentalize and separate topics, whereas feminine leaders will consider a greater number of options and examine them all in relationship to how they'll interact and how they'll affect the costs and benefits of all the different people or groups concerned. Since feminine energy in leadership shows up as a tendency toward collaboration, it often clashes with the decision-making style of the masculine, which is very quick and decisive.*

A truly great leader will know whether a masculine or feminine approach is best for any situation that might arise. And the most effective leader of all will be able to blend both approaches for the very best thought-out and executed decision possible.

Distinction #2: Logic vs. Intuition

Masculine energy is systematic, decisive, and logical. It relies on facts, analytical thinking, and solution-based, problem- fixing approaches. Feminine energy is more anchored in Flow, change, movement, and intuition.

You know you've tapped into your feminine energy when you have a hunch or a sense of knowingness. Author Napoleon Hill, one of the earliest producers of personal success literature, calls it "creative imagination." Those who operate predominantly from their feminine energy do not want to be restricted by a fixed schedule or rigid plan.

The feminine likes to course-correct along the way, changing direction if the path they're on stops feeling right.

Understanding this distinction can go a long way toward ameliorating arguments and disagreements over which problem-solving approach is best. In truth, they are both good and necessary. The trick is in deciding which is most appropriate in the various situations that arise.

For our Flow energy peeps, it is about understanding the power of logic — channeling that creativity, intuition, and vibration into a defined clear container (goal, outcome, target) and analyzing the action plan to manifest it! So we are talking about all that system, detail, timeline massive action kind of stuff.

Are you starting to see the power of combining both these perspectives??? Keep going. There is more where this came from!

Distinction # 3: Result vs. Experience/Impact

Masculine energy is bottom-line results-focused. It's all about crossing that finish line!

Completion is what masculine energy seeks — driving toward and achieving the goal at all cost.

Masculine energy can display traits such as competition, aggression, control, and dominance. How things get done matters less in the world of masculine energy. Although a systematic, logical plan with clearly-defined tasks and a schedule is preferred, getting the outcome is far more important!

Feminine energy, on the other hand, is more about the experience than the outcome. Since the feminine focuses on the collective, the group, the family, or the team, end-results are of less importance than making sure everyone got something out of the journey. The feminine is inspired to create change, especially when an opportunity that benefits the collective shows up. In contrast, the masculine has more of an "if it isn't broke, don't fix it" approach.

In business anything related with the customer experience is usually a field heavily dominated by the feminine. Our economy is more and more relationship-based so this is critical.

Knowledge of this distinction helps give insight to relationship dynamics when one partner is more in the masculine and may just care about a result — and the other more HOW the result is achieved. This understanding is huge and can reduce conflict.

Distinction #4: Masculine Reduces and the Feminine Expands

Masculine energy loves to empty out — to reduce. Where feminine energy loves to expand and fill up!*

Consider this in the area of emotions ... masculine energy is not motivated by nor does it operate on emotions. It prefers to feel less, talk less, and overall seeks to bring things to completion. Where the feminine likes to feel more, talk more, and fill up the space with their energy. This is a great example of how these energies are in contrast.

Let's use the example of communication to show these different energy styles. Feminine uses language in order to express and connect with the other person. In contrast, the masculine uses language specifically to achieve a result, quite often with the goal of fixing something. And for the masculine-energy, the less talking that can be done to achieve this the better!*

Think about that for a moment. There is a huge gap between those two purposes for communicating! Lack of awareness of this distinction leads to countless fights in relationships!

This issue was a huge contributor to the breakdown of my marriage. I wanted to talk simply to express myself, to connect with my husband, and empty out my feelings from the day. Without knowing it, I'd be totally stressing out my masculine-oriented husband, who assumed that the only reason I'd be talking about anything is that I wanted him to solve it for me.

As I talked, he would be interjecting questions based on his need to work out solutions for everything I was venting about.

It never would have occurred to him that I simply wanted to share my experiences with him as a way to feel closer and more connected as a couple.

To him it seemed like there would be no point in me bringing anything up if I weren't asking him to take care of it for me.

As he'd become more stressed as I talked about six different things in one conversation (which he perceived as me looking for a solution on all of them), I'd get less and less comfortable sharing, and eventually clam up.

Consider what happens when you shake a can of pop. That is a great analogy for feminine-core people when they feel like they have to contain their feelings. Eventually I would explode, and then feel utterly deflated and disconnected from my husband. Okay, and yes, I was pissed-off, too. That is my truth! All of that turmoil was simply because we didn't understand the very different ways that feminine-core people and masculine-core people communicate. And we certainly weren't alone. **No one learns this in school or at home!**

We can't expect communication between these two different operating systems to go smoothly until we become educated about them both.

The good news is that once you fully comprehend how differently the feminine and the masculine communicate, you can adjust your own communication style accordingly.

After my husband and I got this part figured out, we set up rules for our conversations wherein everything was clearly defined upfront. *I would say, "Babe, I need to talk." He would respond with, "Are we fixing something, or are you just talking?"* It was remarkable to us both to realize that 90% of the time I would assure him that talking was the fix I was looking for! I wasn't looking for him to solve a problem; I just wanted him to be present and hear me out.

And here's another great tip I strongly suggest. My husband really appreciated it when I would set up a time-expectation for these talks. It can be a difficult experience for someone who's strongly masculine-oriented to sit and listen without agenda and no end in sight!

When I would tell my husband I just wanted ten minutes of his focused attention, he could get excited about offering that to me, because anything with a finite finish-line appeals to masculine energy! For those ten minutes I'd be free to talk, empty, laugh, cry, and end up feeling great, as long as I felt he'd stayed focused on me during my rant. (Feminine energy can detect it if you're thinking about work, or wondering what the score is on the game.)

Understanding this distinction ultimately makes everyone happy. The feminine gets to feel heard, and the masculine gets to be a rock-star simply for showing up.*

I remember the day my husband actually absorbed this nugget of information. He got that "Eureka" expression on his face and said, "I get it now! You're not trying to be logical. You're just talking about how you feel, right?" Bingo! **_Thus began the dance of Hustle and Flow for us!_**

I have shared this with many clients and each time I am equally delighted to hear the success stories and the shock of the masculine male who says ... "you're right; she just wanted me to listen?!?!"

Of course, there were other times when I adjusted my style of communication to better match my husband's. When I wasn't in that space of needing him to listen to me, I could intentionally adjust my communication to meet him in his comfort zone.

Whether you're a man or a woman, masculine energy is fantastic at narrowing down focus, getting at the details, and translating words into action, even though this energy can appear cold or unfriendly when compared to the feminine. It is a great tool when used in the right situation with the right person.

While invaluable within couple dynamics, this communication-style revelation is extremely useful in a work environment as well. If you have leaders or co-workers who operate from their feminine, you might want to try connecting with them beyond simple one-word emails or bullet-point status reports.

For the feminine, every communication exchange is like a deposit into the account of that relationship. They'll value you more if your deposits are similar to theirs. You might notice that instead of quick, bare-minimum voicemails or emails, you get messages with a bit more detail or emotion from feminine-driven people. Meeting the feminine at this level can go a long way toward solidifying relationships and making you more valuable to these people.

When interacting with the feminine, you might want to ask how the weekend was, how the family is, etc. Only do this, however, if you genuinely care. Feminine intuition will spot fake-ness a mile away, and any false attempt at connecting this way will lower your status in the eyes of the feminine. Only use the feminine style of communication if you sincerely desire more rapport and connection with this person.

On the flip side, if you are feminine-energy-oriented and you want to build rapport with a masculine-energy co-worker or boss, you'll want to exhibit a more masculine communication style. That means training yourself to hone in on the most important factors and deliver them clearly and concisely, with no added fluff. To the masculine, effective communication is lean and direct, targeted at solving a problem or making a plan. When was the last time you heard a masculine man get excited about the idea of talking about feelings and emotions?

Masculine communication is quick and to the point with the end goal always in sight. *If it's not broken, then there's no point talking about it!*

One caveat, however — if you normally communicate from a deep feminine energy, and you want to explore this new masculine communication style, you may want to implement these changes gradually. Alternately, tell people that you are exploring a new way of communicating.

When I first went from a feminine communication style to a masculine one, I actually alienated a business partner who felt hurt by my sudden shift. I went from long, chatty Facebook posts and emails to corresponding with bullet points and minimum-word messages. He thought I was upset with him! Once I explained that I was exploring my masculine communication style, he admitted he did appreciate it! He had just read my sudden shift the wrong way.

Of course, the ultimate goal is to become so comfortable with the full spectrum of masculine and feminine energies that you can easily dance between both communication styles depending entirely upon the situation and which style would serve it best. This one point about communication can have a massive impact on your relationships, both personal and in the workplace.

Distinction #5: The Action-Driven Plan vs. the Inspired-Energy Plan

This final distinction is all about results and how they are achieved by the masculine and the feminine. I've repeatedly stressed how masculine energy is focused on getting results, and, of course, that does not mean that the feminine is unconcerned about bringing plans to fruition.

We all want what we want, and we all strive to have our dreams come true in the end. The difference is in the approach.

As I've explained, masculine energy loves schedules, clear focus, and massive action steps. The masculine likes to be time-bound, and the formula is simple: Get clear on what you want and take massive action to get it! These are prized skills in the business world, which is why so many women have become very successful by adopting this area of masculine energy.

I was a Senior Project Manager at one point and spoke in North America and Asia on this topic. Talk about masculine energy! The trouble for me and other women who draw predominately from their masculine, was that I often neglected my true feminine essence because I did not believe it could serve me in creating career results.

I knew that my masculine energy was propelling my career, yet if I really looked at the times I manifested anything truly spectacular, I had to acknowledge that it was my feminine energy that pulled it in. You know the kinds of manifestations I'm talking about — the stuff that makes you call your friend and blurt out, "OMG you will NOT believe what just happened!" Yeah, those off-the-charts experiences just weren't coming out of anything I had scheduled in my day-timer. The juicy and exciting miracles were happening because of my feminine energy.

What I'm talking about now are those synchronicities — those inspired, unplanned actions you take, like when you get a strong feeling to do something illogical and you de-

cide to just do it anyway, and it leads you to something extraordinary. Or, you're thinking about someone completely
random and you decide to call that person out of the blue,
only to find out she unexpectedly has the exact piece of information or resource you've been needing to make something happen.

It's the energetic, vibrational stuff you may want to deny
exists, only you can't deny it because it keeps showing up
in your life.

*I have observed that, without exception, each of
my real fireworks-kind-of opportunities has re-
sulted from me having an energetic plan in addition to my action plan. I'll be going over this in
detail soon, but it's all about harnessing the power of your feminine energy and combining it with
the skills of the masculine.*

So now let's start using this information to create change.
Each chapter will have some "homework" — which include
really key questions to ask yourself so you can start to apply this information in your life.

Chapter Four.
Out of Energetic Alignment?

Let's define this term "energetic alignment" for our use in this book. We have all heard of the topic of "work life balance," right? That is the concept where you are not necessarily trying to live 50% in your work life and 50% in your personal life, but to find an effective balance between the two. It refers to people realizing they are spending too much time in one area (usually their career) and it is having an impact on the quality and results they are getting in their other areas of life — say health, marriage, as a parent, etc.

It is not about where you spend your hours. It's more about the overall quality of life and results you experience.

So the concept here of "work life balance" is not about comparing hours to hours so they equal out; it's more of a conscious focus to include all areas in your life, and depending on the results or experiences you are having in life, you may need to spend more time and focus in one area of life or the other. It will depend on the situation, how you are feeling, or what you are trying to make happen/achieve.

Let's use a similar concept to discuss energies. ***Let's introduce the concept of Energetic Balance.*** The same principle applies where you are not trying to live 50% masculine energy and 50% in feminine, but rather, the recommendation is to live predominately from your core energy (for the majority of women that is Flow and for the majority of men it is Hustle energy).

Now here is what is key to understanding if you are 'out of' or 'in' energetic alignment:

You notice you are out of alignment when the results you are getting, the feelings you are having, and the experiences you are living are not congruent with the life you truly want to live, the way you want to feel, and in a relationship that brings out the best in you.

The question then becomes, ***are you living in energetic alignment?***

Are you using both aspects of your energy — the focus, the action, the logic, the mission driven, and decisive part of you in combination with your compassionate, connecting, intuitive, and energetic part to create results? Or are you living from your opposite energy space and living with the conflict that may cause?

For example, men who operate from their feminine predominately (for most this is not their core energy), will notice quite often they are viewed as the friend and not the romantic interest when it comes to looking for a mate. They don't show up with the polarity that causes attraction in feminine women. They may also be frustrated in their life, not staying on task, and not making the results they want to have happen in their life. They can view that life is happening to them — instead of feeling in charge of their life and taking action to change what is not in line with their purpose or mission.

For women, being out of alignment could show up as not feeling sensual, feeling disconnected from their intuition, overwhelmed, or unable to see a goal to completion.

This subject was covered extensively in a study by the British Psychological Society that defines self-monitoring as the "individuals' ability to accurately assess social situations and to project situational-appropriate responses."

An article referencing the study went on to say, "The researchers used students of an MBA program seven and eight years after their graduation and found that masculine women who were high self-monitors received three times as many promotions as masculine women who were low self-monitors. The high-self-monitoring masculine women also received more promotions than both masculine and feminine men, regardless of the men's self-monitoring abilities."*

You can read the entire study here:

http://www.alphagalileo.org/AssetViewer.aspx?AssetId=4
0772&CultureCode=en

Whether you are in or out of alignment can be narrowed down to this —

- *Is there a gap from where you are now and where you want to be?*

- *Are you using the right energy at the right time?*

- *Are you stuck operating from a space that does not get you the outcome you are looking for?*

- *Are you feeling challenged to connect with others, be a good listener, collaborate, and express yourself in a way that amplifies your business and personal relationships to the next level?*

- *Are you feeling out of control, indecisive, stuck, and a victim of circumstances?*

If there is a gap between the life you are living and the results you are wanting, there are three key areas to address.

1. Your Beliefs

2. How You Manage Your Energy

3. How You Approach Goal Setting

What are Your Beliefs About Using Both Your Hustle and Flow Energy?

Many people fear stepping into their opposite core energy because they are afraid they will over use it, or it will make them less of a man or women. But consider this, if you consciously and intentionally connected with your core energy with daily habits, meaning as a woman you went deeper into owning your radiant femininity and all the powers that come with that ... and as a man you anchor keeping into the roots of your masculinity ... if owning your authentic core energy was part of your very identity and you had daily habits to connect you back to it — *then would you feel more freedom, more permission, and more confidence to switch into the alternative energy?* Because that is exactly what I would like to walk you through in the next few chapters, to give you strategies on how to do this, and to show you the massive impact and positive results it can have on and in many areas in your life!

Are you living predominately from your core energy?

Many conflicts arise internally and then manifest externally when we don't live from our authentic core energy. There are a variety of reasons why this can happen: corporate culture, role modeling as a child, to dynamics in a relationship. However, it is key to connect to and operate from your authentic core energy.

How are You Managing Your Energy in the Moment?

Are you able to decide clearly and decisively the result you want, what the person or project needs, and then bring that aspect out of you to get the job done? Similarly, are you able to shift between your energies effectively?

For example, are you a woman who can optimize your Hustle energy when needed at work, then switch back to your Flow energy when you are on date night with your masculine man?

The next chapter will outline the powerful steps you need to take in order to properly know which energy to bring to the table and how to do it!

How Do You Do Goal Setting?

Are you focused purely with the 'taking massive action' component, leaving all the emotion and vibrational alignment stuff out of the logical picture? Or are you hopping from one spiritual retreat to the next, wondering why you aren't manifesting the experiences of your dreams — secretly hoping meditation and some really good affirmations are all that is needed to do the trick?

Later in this book, I will go into more detail around the Balanced Approach to Goal Setting where we merge both aspects of Doing and Flow to *the most powerful formula for goal setting I have ever experienced!*

If you are ready to use your Hustle plus Flow to create success, and you wouldn't be reading this book if you weren't, let's take this information into your life and begin to get you results NOW!!

Homework

Do you feel that you are in energetic alignment in of your life?

In which areas, if you focused on how you use your Hustle and flow energy, could you be more successful?

Is there an area — Hustle or Flow — that you feel you're not tapping into enough to get the feelings, results, or experience you want?

Is there an energy you are spending too much time in and it is having a negative impact on you?

What areas of your life would improve the most by you learning how to connect deeper at your core energy?

Chapter Five.
How Do You Intentionally Use These Energies?

Now that you understand **WHAT** Hustle and Flow energies are (Chapters 2-3) and **WHY** you want to consciously use your energy (Chapter 4). The next two chapters focus on **HOW** to effectively use these energies to help you become more successful in all areas of your life. This is where it starts to get REALLY exciting!

So, how do you intentionally use these energies? I mean, it sounds like a good idea, right? Much better than just blindly reacting and repeating patterns of behaviour and energy that don't serve you. But how do you take this concept from something you read in a book to application in your life and results in your day to day experiences? How do you use this information to create success in your life, love and business?

Good questions. And this is the exact concern I had when I first dove into this topic. *Interesting info ... now, what do I do with it?*

Well, the first thing you do is use it to become more conscious, more awake in your everyday life, and operate less on autopilot. Whether it came to my relationship with my husband, interactions with women, how I showed up as a leader, as a parent or in business, I started to take a look at how I was showing up. To be honest, most of the time I operated from a pattern — meaning I tended to show up the same way in each situation. Not that this always worked out for me, or for other people very well, I still tended to operate from habit predominately ... only one way of responding — and most of the time during my corporate days it was more like a bull in a china shop wearing heels, lipstick, and a nice dress kind of way.

When I started understanding the different dynamics of energy, my needs, other people's needs, and what it would take to create the reality I wanted, I knew I had to get off the hamster wheel and become more present to each individual moment. I had to make conscious choices to respond not react and to choose the most empowered way to use my energy in the moment for myself and others.

To effectively use the power of Hustle and Flow, it requires you to be tuned into YOU, the people around you, and to the experiences/outcomes you want to bring into your life. You will realize you have more power than you ever dreamed to design your life and what you experience. In order to do that, however, you need to know what you want, and how to show up to get it!

For example, when you understand that the energy you operate from has a huge influence on people and your results, you start to ask yourself some better questions.

As Tony Robbins says:

"Successful people ask better questions, and as a result, they get better answers."*

And you use these better answers to guide your energy and actions. Your Hustle and Flow. You start to become more conscious, more on purpose, and more present in each moment. This chapter will outline six steps you use to effectively manage your energy in the moment and when interacting with people. The next Chapter will focus on how to use your energy for goal setting and creating results.

Let's dive into the six steps. First, we will start at the beginning with your mindset. Recreating powerful versions of your Hustle and Flow Identities — because without these we will merely repeat more of the same results! We will then move on and talk about areas such as leading from our energetic core, when to switch between Hustle and Flow, our energetic blind spots, Relationships, Communication, and daily habits to deepen your connection to your authentic core energy.

So, go get a beverage of your choice, a pen and paper (yes we are going old school here), and let's get started! You can also find many print outs and exercises on my website, *www.LisaToste.com.*

Step 1: Your Hustle and Flow Identities 2.0 Version

"Where did these beliefs about who I am come from, and how old are they?" Tony Robbins*

How are you defining your Hustle Identity and Flow Identity?

Are they empowering definitions or are they disempowering? It is critical to understand your blueprint in this area as it either sets you up for success, defeat, or possibly LOTS of internal conflict.

Have you ever considered what your beliefs and rules are about your Hustle and Flow side? Where did they come from anyway? How old are they? When were they last updated?

I heard a great saying once that most of our technology is more updated then our belief systems ... sadly, I would agree!

Consider that many of us have picked up our beliefs from our parents, culture, and society and never even questioned if these beliefs served us or represented how our model of the world REALLY works. Often, many of our beliefs were created when we were young.

When is the last time you took a look at how you view feminine FLOW energy? Or Masculine HUSTLE energy?

What you may have believed about these traits, values, and behaviours at one time may no longer be true. Holding on to these beliefs may also harm you, your relationships, and you overall success. I heard Tony Robbins make this powerful statement once and it had a huge impact on me...

"The strongest Force in the human personality is the need to stay consistent with how we define ourselves."

So how we DEFINE OURSELVES — all parts of ourselves — is key, because it can limit us or set us free.

By identity, I'm referring to an aspect of you. We all have different identities within us. For example, we have the identity of who we are as a spouse (nurturing, protective and passionate wife), a friend (I am the wild, crazy, loyal and fun friend), and identity for who we are at work (resourceful, result-focused go-getter).

An identity is made up of beliefs, stories, experiences, and associations you pick up in life. Identities are not made in stone, given to you at birth, or unchangeable. Thankfully they are very adaptable, which is how people grow and evolve. It does, however, take a conscious effort to do so.

If there is a version of the Hustle or Flow part of you that didn't serve you in the past, great news! Let's update it now! Let's run a new software operating system that can now rewrite limiting beliefs and set the foundation for you to feel more comfortable about stepping into each energy consciously, intentionally, and with purpose. And, to ensure we have a powerful connection to our core energy (the space we resonate with most and live from more often).

Now, I'm not saying that I have a magic wand and by doing this exercise, it will obliterate overnight some strong association or ties you have to old conditioning. What I am saying is this is a massive exercise to create congruency and momentum within you — to focus and use these energetic parts of yourself with intention to get the best results or experience. This exercise will get you to examine and re-choose your beliefs, so you can truly say your version of Flow energy is one you created, one that serves you and your dreams ... not something society dictated to you — a version that may have MANY limiting beliefs holding you back from using it!

Without having these identities for both your Hustle and your Flow, this whole energy topic stays intellectual and outside of you and would not allow you to do the upcoming exercises from the most powerful space.

I really want you to embody this, test this, tweak it, and make this your own. From the bottom of my heart, I truly want you to use the dynamic information in this book to create positive change, results, and the experiences in your life you crave, so that you can enjoy your version of SUCCESS!

And, don't worry. I will walk you through it. Consider these identities as the version of the devil and angel sitting on your shoulder ... well, similar to that, without the whole negative devil bit!

Just two identities on your shoulders, ready to assist you whenever needed with different values, behaviours, and energies as their tools. One wearing Prada (FLOW representing style, beauty, grace — and yes they have a men's line so again nothing to do with gender!), and one wearing Nike (HUSTLE energy — Just do it!). Again, just checking with you that we're not stuck in the gender trap here!

Okay let's dig deep here!!!

Flow Energy Identity

Write down your answers to these questions:

Now that you know more about the power of Flow, what current beliefs or stories about feminine Flow energy would you need to let go of or change?

For example, Flow energy is only appropriate for women. Or Flow traits are not as powerful at making things happen as Hustle energy is. Consider all those limits. What would you have to let go of to allow a more powerful version of Flow to become a part of you?

What beliefs would you need to take on in your life to allow you to deepen your connection and allow you to powerfully use Flow energy in your life?

How would your life be impacted if you were even more intuitive, connected, empathetic, focused on the collective good for everyone, and the power of relationships?

How would being powerfully feminine impact your life?

How would this impact either your current intimate relationship or your ability to attract a new one?

If you are Flow at your core, would this increase your attraction from you mate?

If you are Hustle at your core, would this allow you to be more compassionate, a better listener, and meet some needs of your mate more?

How would this impact your career?

If you are Feminine at your core, how could you embrace this space even more, knowing you had masculine energy available to use whenever you needed it? The next step will be to create your **2.0 Hustle Identity Flow**. Knowing you can access your Hustle — does this allow you to deepen your connection and use of your Flow?

If you are masculine at your core, how could developing this Flow energy within you create even better results in your life?

If you have not been deeply connected and used Flow energy consciously and effectively in your life, what has it cost you?

What is now possible for you because of your new awareness, sorting through your beliefs, stories and connecting to a deeper state of Flow?

What action can you take right now to acknowledge, appreciate, or affirm your connection to your Flow energy?

WHEW!!! Those were some big questions! Did you write the answers in? Come on, do the work and get the rewards! Did these questions cause you to focus on your current identity of FLOW? Did you notice a shift in your perspective just by questioning yourself in these areas?

Great! Now you have this newly updated flow force that you can use in the next few steps and as you go about your life! Well done!

Now it's time to update the software for our Hustle Identity. Give these questions a try! There is no right or wrong answer. The intention is to become more aware of this important aspect of yourself ... to make it feel and become more a part of who you are. Because, well, it already is!

Now on to the next energy!

Hustle Energy Identity

Now that we know more about the power of Hustle, what current beliefs or stories about masculine Hustle energy would you need to let go of or change? For example, 'Hustle energy is only appropriate for men.' Or, 'Our Hustle traits are not as aligned with making things happen in a spiritual way because they are about forcing something to happen.'

What would you have to let go of to allow a more powerful version of Hustle become a part of you?

What beliefs would you need to take on in your life to allow you to connect and allow you to powerfully use Hustle energy in your life?

Knowing that you are connecting more to your Hustle — does this help you if you are a woman?

How would your life be impacted if you had the ability to tap into even more focus, decision making, time management, and on your individual needs?

How would having access to being powerfully 'Hustle,' impact your life?

How would this impact either your current intimate relationship or your ability to attract a new one?

If you are Hustle at your core, would this increase your attraction from your mate?

If you are Flow at your core, would this allow you to communicate your individual needs better, set boundaries, and go after what you wanted in a relationship?

How would being more in the Hustle-zone impact your career?

If you are Feminine at your core, would having daily habits to anchor you back to your Flow energy help you to reduce any fear of getting STUCK in your Masculine state?

If you are Feminine at your core, how could developing this feminine energy within you create even better results in your life?

If you have not been deeply connected and used Hustle energy consciously and effectively in your life, what has it cost you?

What is now possible for you because of your new awareness and sorting through your beliefs, stories and connecting to a deeper state of Hustle for you?

What actions can you take right now to acknowledge, appreciate, or affirm your connection to your Hustle energy?

Fabulous work!

Now let's put these new identities to work! We'll now get into the five other steps in understanding how to manage and shift between your energies for the results or experiences you are looking to create and achieve.

Step 2: Lead from Your Core Energy

Now that you have powerfully new Hustle and Flow identities, you can learn to switch between them depending on the needs of the situation. It is vital, however, that you base this shifting of your energy from the foundation of your core energy — the space you will want to live, connect to daily and operate from your core most of the time. Lead and approach each situation from this perspective, then view how the alternative energy can better serve or complement the end goal or experience. This is where your true power, authenticity, and gifts reside.

What we are speaking about here is going deeper into who you are a woman or man at your core.

Appreciate, own, and operate from your core energy most of the time. Approach your situations, relationships and goal setting from this perspective first. Consider it your foundation. If you are Flow at your core (as most women are), engage in the influence of these values, traits, and behaviours first. Bring these energetic dynamics as your first responders to the scene, so to speak.

For a visual example, consider a little ambulance-type truck pulling up as you arrive at a situation, meeting, or are approaching a new goal. The first people to come out of this imaginary truck (no idea why, but these characters look like Lego® figurines to me!), are your core energy peeps. They assess the scene to see what support they can bring to the situation first before calling for backup.

Let me give you a personal example. Often in my previous corporate life, I was the only female (my core energy is FLOW) in the room. In order to fit in, I often made the mistake of becoming LIKE the other people in the board room who listened to 99.5 ALL HUSTLE ALL DAY ABSOLUTELY NO COMMERCIAL BREAKS FOR FLOW EVER FM radio. SO I dialed my energy to that station. Now sometimes that was great. But truly I was missing a great opportunity to use my FLOW traits, behaviours, and gifts that would have added even more to the discussion. Using this Step of Leading from your authentic core — I started to approach meetings first from my Flow state, and asked some great questions to myself:

Does someone need to connect or be heard? How can collaborating achieve the resolution in a win/win dynamic? What items need to be multi-tasked in order to allow an outcome to be reached? Is there a feeling or sense of what's the right way to handle a situation? What is the overall feeling in the room?

These are a few examples of great questions your FLOW first responder peeps would use to scope out a situation. Once I operated from this space, then I could also switch to the alternative dynamics that may also be needed in this mix. For example, if there is a time sensitive action that needs to happen in order to meet a deadline, you also may have to add a few splashes of focus, problem solving, decision making, and time management to the blend.

What I'm getting at is not to deny or immediately overlook the value your core energy brings to the table.

Are you getting the point here? Because this is big!

It doesn't have to be one or the other. You can inspire and drive from both places.

You may want to start by collaborating, listening to all the ideas in the room, and do a check on how you feel intuitively, but set a time limit that a 3:00pm decision is being made and action will be taken to meet the deadline.

Using that combo gets you the best of both worlds. By approaching the situation from your Flow core first, you are approaching it from a more authentic and empowered place.

Second, you're not leaving your natural traits, perspectives, and values on the table. You're simply addressing it right off-the-bat. You can administer Hustle style action, but from a flow foundation. There are alternative and innovative ways in handling situations that come about from doing exactly this!

The same goes if you are Hustle at your core. Initially approach and assess the situation from a masculine perspective.

When the Lego figurines pop out of the truck, they may ask questions like, "What is the problem that needs to be solved? What do I need to do to get results? What is the challenge I need to overcome?" This is a solid and grounded place for Hustle energy. From here you can also consider the Flow perspective, "Who else do I need to help me with this outcome? Do I have a hunch at what the next right action should be? Who will be impacted by the decisions? Will talking with or collaborating with someone specific help my planning?" This is a very balanced approach, yet the Hustle essence is not lost or less than. This Hustle foundation couples with just the right amount of Flow dynamics to increase optimal results.

Honour your core energy.

You were designed with that as your home base for a reason. The ability to shift into the opposite energy is intended to allow you to relate better with other people and evolve in your dynamics as a soul in this world. If, however, you do this by leaving your home energy, you will lose your authenticity. You'll see this in your results and it will be felt by others.

Have you ever been around someone and just felt like something was off or they weren't genuine? This is the feeling you get when someone is not operating from their core space. We have all been there and done that on occasion — well, at least I certainly have!

There is no blame in it. Just an opportunity to realize there is a way to step up your game, and that is to be as authentic to who you are as much as possible.

Shed any stereotypes, marketing campaigns you've seen, or even your parents' idea of masculine and feminine, if they do not serve your authenticity. Embrace the true essence of your home energy and all it has to offer you and the world.

The deeper and more connected you are to your core energy, the easier it will be for you to step into and use your other complimentary energy. Mainly because your fear of being STUCK in the opposite energy (and the cost of doing that), are not a concern.

The last step in the six-step process is to honour and connect back to your home energy daily. We will outline different daily habits and rituals you can use to connect deeper to your Feminine FLOW or you Masculine HUSTLE daily.

For this step — really consider:

How and what would change in your life if you initially approached each situation from your authentic core energy?

What energy state do you generally lead with? Is it different at work then it at home or socially? Or is it always the same? Why?

Consider, how would your relationships be impacted if you lead from your core space first?

How would your work environment be impacted?

What are your top 3-5 questions you can use to guide your focus in a situation to lead with your core?

Conduct an experiment. Take your questions from the previous page and bring them into your life for the next five days.

Use them to guide you in both work, home, and social situations. See the impacts! Maybe they will inspire new questions and patterns.

Step 3: Know When You May Need to Switch Energetic Lanes

As important as knowing the glory and awesomeness of your core energy, you also may want to understand the blind spots. This will help you to understand why you may be having challenges in relationships, achieving your goals, or feeling juiced and empowered in your life.

Masculine Hustle and Feminine Flow energies are called complementary energies because they do just that — complement the other — Yin and Yang.

One energy blind spot is the strength of the opposite energy. They work fantastically and effectively together.

This is another great reason why trying to live from one energy exclusively does not create as much success. For example, a man avoiding his FLOW qualities or a woman shaming herself from ever using Hustle traits. This can place you at a disadvantage by not dancing between your Yin and Yang!

The information following will help outline the strengths and blind spots of each energy.

Remember when we discussed showing up in your authentic core energy most of the time, and then checking in to see if that was helping you to get the results you were looking to experience and achieve?

And, if you were blocked or not getting your results, you could engage the opposite energy. The following information will help you understand the most common blindspots of each energy and WHEN you most likely will need to turn on your energetic indicator lights and switch energy lanes!

Flow Energy Strengths and Blind Spots — The Art of Being

Strengths

There are MANY strengths to the energy of FLOW. Often these are overlooked and under used. There are a number of reasons why this powerful energy is not used to its full potential yet. One of the reasons is that it has been linked exclusively to the gender of women. I am going to skip the obvious history lesson here outlining how female traits had been diminished and deemed weak in society. Since this book is asking you to suspend the gender labels, we can have this discussion with fresh eyes. A discussion which will help both men and women use FLOW energy in a way to take their ability to be successful to a whole new level!

The good news is that I do think society is starting to recognize the necessity of this energy for both men and women in all areas of life, love, and even business. Yes, you read the last word right! *I am coaching companies and individuals on how to use the gifts of FLOW in their business.* It is a key element in leadership, team culture, client relationships, and peak performance of individuals. If you look at top performers in different industries you will notice they have yoga, meditation, spiritual practices, and employ many qualities of Flow dynamics. Many of them may be HUSLTE at their core — yet they understand and employ the power of Flow to increase their success!

Now, if you are already FLOW at your core and anchor deeper to it, image the possibilities?

Another reason people underuse the energy of FLOW is their ability to understand and use these traits. For example, the power of intuition is incredible. More and more people are acknowledging the reality of this sixth-sense, while others have been operating with this guidance for years. Meditation, connection to inner guidance, intuition, the ability to feel and use the power of energy to create, are a few strengths of flow energy. These are the opposite of the logical, more touch-and-see focus of the Hustle energy.

Operating from a space of being able to feel, know, and understand that life is energy and it is powerful. Inspired action — you know those things you do because you got this idea out of "nowhere?" Like taking a different route home from work one day and bumping into a new love interest? This actually happened to a friend of mine and she married the guy she bumped (more like smashed), into. This dance of synchronicity, following an inner guidance — these are key strengths.

Have you ever heard someone say they were "in the FLOW"?

Well, they were referring to a mystical and exhilarating unraveling of events that lead them to their desired outcome.

Other traits can be found in chapter 3, however, a summary can be described by the ability to focus on the group, the collective consciousness, and to connect with more than the eye can see ...

Overall FLOW brings an infusion of life force that can be felt when it enters a room.

It instills passion, joy, beauty, and possibility into all situations. The ability to feel so deeply is key in their ability to line up their vibration and make things happen. We will go into specifics in the next chapter on **HOW** to do this! Overall, the strengths of FLOW energy are undeniable when it comes to creating success, if you can also manage the blind spots.

Blind Spots

Like any strength — it comes with some blind spots. If you can become aware of them, and put some strategies in place to compensate for them, they will increase your ability to effectively create your life. When I work with many clients who are FLOW energy at their core, these are common challenges we work through. By adding a sprinkle of Hustle energy to compensate, you can turn these challenges to breakthroughs!

Focus on Self

Often Flow peeps are so focused on the needs of others (friends, family, co-workers, clients, etc.), we often forget to take care of ourselves. Burn out, resentment, and giving up on our dreams are often the result. I have experienced all three — been there, done that, and bought the t-shirt-making factory! The reality is this, and as annoying as this may sound — ***we need to make our self a priority***. I say it sounds annoying because the next question that comes up when you read this may be — HOW? I have so much to do, so many people are counting on me that I just cannot make time for me!

The truth of this is you cannot give, create impact, or create the life you want without taking care of you!

We all know that self-care can take many forms (eating, exercising, relaxing — yes you read that right take time JUST FOR YOU!), but one you may not have thought of — that is, more of a Hustle-type of self-care is to call out your personal success and celebrations.

Many people who are HUSTLE core energy have a much easier time calling out their individual successes in the work place. This is one of the reasons cited for people more comfortable in their Hustle energy getting recognition and promotions. *Simply having someone say, "Well done!" can do wonders for how we feel.*

Decision Making

Because Flow peeps can see and care about how a decision can impact other people, there can be a reluctance to make a decision and move forward. Flow energy allows the ability to see so many possibilities, to want to get input from people, and decide from a place of most positive impact. This can cause delays in action and procrastination. Flow peeps can find the action of making a final decision, with specific details, clarity, and moving forward, not so much fun to say the least. It is not that they don't have the ability, more because they care so deeply that they get it right for everyone involved. This can be daunting.

To help you move forward, a little dose of Hustle energy is required. Ask yourself some key questions to drill down on what YOU really want (yes you, Flow peep — your needs count). Check out the first step in the next chapter to provide you with a format on how to help you in the Decision Making process.

Time Management

Yes, we have got to say the "S" word here … Scheduler. Time Management can be a challenge for Flow energy — I mean look at the word FLOW — the opposite of rigid schedule. I get it, and here is the thing — managing your time is key.

Doing this right can help you with making time for you (see how I snuck that in there?) Yes, self-care is that important.

It's not so much HOW you manage time, it's more that you can play with it. A term I love is *fluid structure.* Meaning, you find your balance between structure and the ability to be in the flow.

Consider that what is key is knowing your outcome, what and when you want to make something happen. Allow for inspired action to also play in your scheduler. Allow time for you to break up your day of action and scheduled focus time, with some FLOW time. For example, during the week my scheduler is PACKED with back-to-back meetings, coaching calls, getting my kids to school, dinner, homework time,, etc.! You get the point. But there is NO WAY I would do any of that without some breaks of Flow injected into that focused, time sensitive action packed day! I would be a nightmare to be around if I didn't!

Even writing this book — sitting and focusing is, well, not my idea of a good time, to be honest. So, for all things I have 10-15 minute Dance breaks! LOL — you may laugh, but you know how good that feels when you have hard core Hustling all day.

So, in between my Actions, I use music to medicate me! Singing, moving, dancing ... all that is my true way to survive. Essential oils a beautiful element to work in, and phone calls to laugh with my BFF are all in my day plan! It is amazing for my creativity, my energy, and overall how I show up with people. I give many of my clients music-related homework — don't knock it till you try it! If you can setup 30 -45 minutes of focused time and then inject a few minutes of flow break, you will be amazed and how your productivity can skyrocket!

Taking Action

Don't get me wrong. FLOW energy does a lot, and usually all at the same time! Multi-tasking, taking care of everyone needs — yes flow peeps are doing a lot. Yet, are they doing it in a way that serves THEM?

The lack of focus on taking care of their needs, making a timely decision based on that, and not managing their time to get what THEY want are caps on results. For someone operating exclusively from 103.5 FLOW FM all day every day, they are not dialed into their highest version of success.

What is interesting is that self-focus, making a decision, time management, and taking action are key components of Hustle energy!

You can see how and why these energies are called complimentary now right?

Hustle Energy Strengths and Blind Spots — The Science of Doing

Strengths

The power of Hustle energy is easy to describe now — it is the opposite of what you just read! The main focus is on taking care of the individual's needs/goals and taking logical steps to make them happen!

This energy is the main focus on which the corporate business world of command and control has been based. This is one reason people who operate from a place of Hustle traits are so successful in business. The focus on protecting, having a , and staying focused on purpose, make for an amazing tool kit of energy from which everyone can benefit.

Blind Spots

Using Feelings to create: As mentioned in chapter 3, Hustle energy likes to reduce — talk less, feel less, etc. The challenge is that feelings can be used as fuel and they have the power to help you create! In chapter 6, we go into detail on how to use your feelings/emotions to help you align your vibration. This is a powerful means for creation.

If your feelings are cutoff or you reduce them, it will impact your relationships and your ability to connect with others — in life, business, or to yourself.

There is a balance of being grounded and feeling your emotions. You can use and direct your emotions to help you be successful — not to have them use you and feel out of control. Feelings are the cornerstone of Flow energy. You can see how add this energy will help you with all the above! Connecting deeply to your reasons for WHY you do anything is essential for any type of success!

Looking Within

The essence of Hustle masculine energy is outward focused. The "when I see it, I will believe it" could be a tag line for Hustle energy. It is about the here and right NOW NOW NOW!

Often quieting the mind, going inward, and connecting to either your inner silence or an aspect you feel empowered by (be this source, the universe, God, or whatever name you use), is a key ingredient. It is often the "edge" (yes I am using Hustle lingo here), that makes all the difference in your life!

The ability to use an inner guidance — one that is not backed up with empirical date and logical, is exactly what can help you UP the miracle-factor in your life.

Everything is Connected

This is actually true. This is not just a nice warm feeling kind of idea. It is more rooted in quantum physics that we are connected far beyond our current level of science can even understand! We are far more energy than we are matter — that being said, we are all connected.

To take the idea further, Hustle energy can sometimes be short-sighted in the here, now, and me!

Even further, it is to take into consideration the needs of the greater good, the group — to take into decision making how one's action impacts other people and things — to consider how this would impact our environment, our economy, political systems and how food is grown.

These areas are currently dominated by Hustle thought processes which can be great for bottom line profits, yet not so great for the impact of society. For Hustle energy, it can be a blind-spot to not view the connectedness of actions and decisions on others.

Listening and Communication

Hustle energy reduces, right? Well, nowhere else, other than in communication, can this be so obvious! Quick, short communication gets to the point and makes things happen quickly. That is perfect for getting results, unless you are trying to communicate with Flow peeps.

When trying to build connection, rapport, or inspire trust and leadership, less may not be a good thing. Step 5 gives you very clear guidance on how to speak with both Hustle and Flow energy so to avoid repeating (which Hustle energy would HATE — I will have you refer to step 5 for more details on the how).

For the intention of this part of the book, what is important is to understand listening and communication may be a blind-spot for Hustle energy, especially when interacting with authentic Flow-core people.

Consider the following:

What blind-spots do you recognize from your own life that stop you from being as successful as you want to be?

What strategy can you put in place to help you overcome this blind-spot? How can using the complimentary energy help you do that?

What empowering questions can you use to help turn this blind-spot into a strength?

Step 4: The Power of Polarity

Polarity is used to describe what happens when two opposite energies interact. Think about two magnetized pieces. When you have a negatively and a positively charged magnet coming close to each other, what happens? BOOM. They snap together in an energetic field you can feel occurs, pulling them together. Another example can be seen in the chemistry of two people when they meet ... or the lack of it! When two magnets are put together that are like-energy (say positive and positive), they repel each other. An equally strong force field can be felt pushing these pieces together.

Passion is Created by Polarity

For example, when you have a man deeply connected and operating from his Hustle energy, and a woman deeply connected and operating from authentic Flow energy, a powerful connection occurs.

What happens with some couples is that over time, the polarity weakens. They start hanging out all the time, doing the same activities, and they become close friends. The differences in preferences, activities, and energy, which made them polar to each other, slips away and now the passion fizzles. This can also be known as the slippery slope of the "jogging suit phase."

This is a critical topic when discussing Masculine Women and Feminine Men and how it translates into relationship issues.

Passion is fuelled by contrasting energies. Knowing when to turn the dial up on your core energy to increase the passion is a great tool to increase the spice in your love life or for elements of romantic attraction overall.

When it comes time to know when to dance between your Hustle and Flow, and if you're looking to create a spark or passion, then polarize your energy with your person of interest or mate.

Relationships

I mentioned before that the pivotal point for me came from the turnaround I experienced in my own personal relationship. I was on the verge of divorce. This was my "now I've tried everything" last attempt. My husband and I did love each other. It was just the day-to-day stresses and a lack of polarization that had taken its toll. Truly, at that time that was our only challenge — but that seemed to infect every aspect of our relationship. Our chemistry was the WHY we had come together as a couple — so when that faded this impacts were huge.

I tested this polarity thing. And it worked, but here is the HUGE key — *you need to polarize despite how your partner may be showing up*. Let me translate that into an example. If your partner who is Hustle at his core, is showing up either with too much masculinity (cold, focused only on himself, and his needs) or to little masculine energy (dull, hopeless, lacks mission, focus), then it may not feel safe or intuitive for you to go into a feminine Flow state.

How he is showing up may trigger you to go into your masculine Hustle — to balance out the lack of masculinity in your relationship (due to the insufficient amount he is bringing to the dynamic, or to put up a defensive barrier between you and his overly-masculine Hustle behaviour).

Incidentally, I am ONLY referring to healthy, non-abusive relationships here. I am in no way recommending to go into your feminine Flow to solve any problems that are related to abuse in ANY form.

With that said, let me highlight again that although you may not feel like dressing up for him and looking beautiful, being in your Flow, putting down the masculine barriers and just being an energetic feminine woman, that is precisely the step you want to test out. Everything is energy.

People in relationships can get into energetic patterns of how they relate.

So imagine if you, as I did, just shook it up and showed up completely different. Not because your couple's therapist told you or you were "trying" to work things out. Rather, you just decided to show up in your most powerful authentic self in your core state.

This is most likely the state in which your relationship started and where you were when it was at its hottest, sexiest, and fulfilling.

This is what I did, and I decided I would do this for sixty days ... without telling my husband what I was doing, just going deeper into my Flow energy for me and to see the impacts it had on us.

Well, without going into too many details here, it worked out really well and we are celebrating thirteen years together at the time of writing this book.

I am not saying Hustle and Flow energy dynamics are at the core of all marriage issues, or that they will save all marriages from divorce. BUT, I am saying ... they are at the core of many. I can honestly say that for the challenges I was going through at that time, understanding the concepts in this book changed the dynamics of our marriage.

Consider these questions:

How could you go deeper into your core energy to spark more attraction with your mate or to attract one?

What beliefs, habits, or fears are holding you back?

How would your relationship be impacted if you were able to play more full out from this core space, intentionally, to create more passion in your relationship. or to seek one?

Step 5: Communication — Recognize and Meet the Needs of Others Energy

"To effectively communicate, we must realize that we are all different in the way we perceive the world and use this understanding as a guide to our communication with others." Tony Robbins*

When you can understand the needs of both Hustle and Flow energy, you can meet the needs of other people and better communicate your needs. This will make a huge impact on every relationship you have, whether personal or professional.

A fabulous example can be seen in the area of communication — which is the cornerstone of any relationship. It either creates trust, intimacy, and sense of being understood or, it can isolate, create misunderstandings, and be the reason for the relationship's breakdown.

Understanding someone else's communication style can create a huge advantage. Consider this in your career whether with a client, co-worker, or leader. If they are more Hustle energy, they will prefer to reduce things — like words! Offer quick to-the-point bullets of information focused on the required action or the solution. A long, descriptive email or talk would be more flow in nature and less appealing.

Now consider the opposite. If your leader, manager, or client is more Flow in nature, then you would be better off connecting first before jumping into business. To be more relationship-focused, present options, and have more details available to them.

When researching this topic, I found the issue of communication to be a top-ranked reason for divorce (usually ranking in the top 1-3),* or for breakups.

Whether we are talking about working relationships, intimate relationships, or family, communication is the foundation.

The ability to understand someone's communication style and meet those needs will hugely impact many facets of your life!

Key Strategies for Communicating with Someone in their Hustle or Flow State

A summary of Flow State communication looks ... like a lot of talking. Remember in an earlier chapter when we talked about Hustle energy reduces and Flow Energy expands? Well, now more than ever, is that statement true then in the area of communications!

Flow communication is very expressive, emotional. It is a form of bonding, emptying emotions, and moving energy. It is critical for Flow energy to feel HEARD. So, for anyone getting this element of listening wrong, this spells disaster in a relationship.

Below are a few key points that will help increase your success in communication and positively impact your relationships.

So before we go into this again, remember the ground rules here:

Remember we are not talking about gender. And people don't always communicate in the same style — most of the time they will have patterns. And, how someone communicates at work, under stress, or with friends, may be different.

Key Strategies for Speaking with Flow Energy

Avoid opening the shaken pop can — also known as — let her talk and don't interrupt her with solutions or strategies.

As we discussed earlier, one of the main challenges I had with my relationship was our communication. I would talk (just to express my emotions, kind of get it out of me and to share how I was feeling; very Flow qualities), and my very masculine man would misunderstand this for me wanting him to FIX something.

So as I would speak, he would be searching for an answer.

During this I could feel a lack of his presence ... which would, well ... piss me off. And then he would come up with solutions to items I was not looking to fix ... I was just talking about them. This of course made no sense to my Hustle energy man.

Give Her What She Wants/Needs, Not What You Think She Should Need

This is one of the hiccups masculine Hustle energy peeps can have when dealing with Flow energy. For example, the predominately Hustle energy man will want to take care of a feminine Flow woman, and in doing so, sometimes they don't LISTEN to what Flow feels they need (which at times can seem illogical to Hustle energy because it may be based on feelings not analysis) — and instead gives them what the masculine energy THINKS they need to fix a problem.* Yes ... that will get you in hot water quickly. My husband and I have gone over this little bump in the road many, many times. It is all done from a place of love and wanting to take care, yet the results can be a disaster if a woman feels unheard.

Understand This May Not Be A Quick Conversation

Remember that FLOW energy likes to expand things — especially in communication — so just know speaking with someone in their Flow state (man or woman) that it is not going to be a quick chat. And, if you need it to be, use guided questions. Direct the person to make decisions or give you the info you need ... and understand that Flow energy hates to be rushed!

Yes. One Topic is Related to Another in the Energy of Flow

Hustle energy is great at compartmentalizing. Where, for Flow energy, one thing is connecting to another ... it does not have to make logical sense ... it just is.

Everything is connected.

At times this can be frustrating to a Hustle peep. Consider though that Flow energy is concerned with the needs of the group and considering all the options. One decision does impact others — and a Flow energy brain cannot help but make the connections. Questions that are meant to be answered with a yes or a no — most likely will also have a story or conversation around them because everything is connected!

Key Strategies for Speaking with Hustle Energy

If it cannot be fixed now — if you don't have a solution, why are we talking about it? Hustle energy likes to DO, FIX, and SOLVE problems.* Conversation for the sake of chit-chat is not high in priority.

Do NOT Hint — Just Say What You Want!

When I was dating my husband, he said something very profound and honestly, it stuck with me and modified our communication pattern right from the start.

He asked me to never hint. I laugh even recalling this conversation — he was very clear that he was crap at figuring out what I hinting at (of course I felt completely valid in expecting him to read my mind, which of course seems a little off now that I think about it).

He said that if you want me to get or fix something, fine I can do it ... just TELL ME. Do not hint. Honestly that is some really good advice there!

He actually means what he said ... really!

Not so many words — get to the point. Communication has a focused result in mind for Hustle energy. Hustle communication is very results-focused and to the point. So bullet point emails that clearly point out What the ASK is, what the Answer is, or what is the Key point of the communication, the better!!!

Hustle Does NOT Need to Talk — It Actually Can Make a Person More Stressed

Flow energy needs to speak. ... Hustle energy does not.

This can be really hard for FLOW peeps to understand.

Many times we can think someone is mad or upset because they are not speaking ... no. Speaking does not fill the same need for Hustle energy that it does for Flow energy. That is it ... seriously. Wild I know!

When I ask my husband, who is a brilliant man — what are you thinking about? When he says nothing — get this ... he means it!?! Can you imagine that? If you are Flow at your core like me, you can't. Sigh ... and, I bet it is awesome!

Consider how you can use the above information to become more successful now with your communication. Answer the following questions:

What are two ways you can improve your communication with your mate, friends, or family today?

What point or points above on communication would be important to let your mate, friends, or family know about you, to improve how they communicate with you?

What could you do to improve your communications with people at work or in your business?

Step 6: Come Back Home to Your Core Energy Again!

Some people fear that by switching into the other contrasting energy, the dance between masculine and feminine, they'll lose their essence or go off-balance for too long. They fear they may become Masculine Women or Feminine Men who get stuck operating from their opposite core energy and stay in it for all situations.

For example women may fear getting stuck operating from a Hustle space and it impacting their relationship, as I did. Similarly, a male can fear getting stuck operating from Flow space and losing the ability to polarize his energy enough attract a lover.

They may get stuck in the doomed friend zone because the chemistry of polarized energy (remember the magnets) never produces a spark — let alone a whole fire!

My suggestion is to make connecting to your core energy both a daily and scheduled routine.

Yes, Flow peeps! I did just say the dreaded "S" word again— Schedule!

I acknowledge that "scheduling" time to align with your feminine flow energy seems a little Hustle in nature, but consider the alternative.

When life gets hectic and stress levels start to climb, many women get caught in the trap of handling life from a masculine Hustle perspective. I did and so do many of my clients.

When men feel emasculated and try to cope by showing up in their feminine, they too can get caught up in the pattern of living in the opposite energy.

How to Connect to Your Core Flow State

"Both masculine and feminine approaches have strengths and limitations. When an organization is dominated by either masculine or feminine approaches, there is a risk that the downsides of that approach will emerge. With a balance of masculine and feminine approaches, the organization gets more of the strengths and less of the downsides of each."*

When I work with clients there are key homework assignments we focus on between the calls to get them more connected and anchored to Flow and Hustle energy. There are many wonderful ways to do this — here are my* top five suggestions!

Move it! — Dance (my favourite). Listen to your favourite music and move, dance! Go for walks, do yoga — move your wonderful body! Between my writing, coaching, and speaking (yes in front of my audience I do this), I make sure there are dance breaks. Try this. It feels like a great stress release and great connection to the body. Flow is about movement, change, and the body.

Self-care and your senses — Take bubble baths with candles, music, and dark chocolate! Yummy. I am already teaching my 5-year-old daughter this is how to replenish and give back to yourself. Take time to take care of you! Truly, we cannot be successful unless we make this activity a MUST in our routine. Bringing yourself out of your mind and the 1,001 things you need to DO — focus it back on being, feeling, and enjoying the moment.

Meditate — Take time alone, meditation, praying, connecting to the non-physical. Connect within and to a higher source (I am not here to tell you what to name that source, but connecting to something beyond). The ability to tune out the external world and go inward is key to connecting with your flow and I highly suggest starting and ending your day this way. Even 15 minutes morning and night will make a huge difference. Test it and see!

Connect to your intuition — Feminine Flow is so connected to universal energy and the magic of our intuition. It's the ultimate sense of being connected and aligned ... to cut yourself off from it is to cut yourself off of the core essence of Flow. Doing the above activity of going inward will help you establish your intuition even more. Trust it and cultivate it. This one component can significantly improve your ability to create results in anything you do.

Dress to make YOU feel beautiful — Yes, yoga and active gear is comfortable — but dressing beyond the comfortable and expressing your own beauty — for yourself, is a delicious expression of Flow. It is that radiance, grace, and feeling of emotion expressed. Another positive side to this is when you feel beautiful you are experienced by others as more confident, sexy, and interesting ... so I say go for it!

How to Connect to Your Core Hustle State

Keeping in line with the energy traits — there seems to be MANY more options when discussing connecting to Flow vs. connecting to Hustle energy.

1) Connect to the physical; working out.

2) Focus on results, the end game. Set objectives for yourself with specific times and dates for completion.*

3) Do activities that drive competition, individual results, or action.*

4) Focusing on your purpose and continuing to take massive action towards fulfilling your mission.

5) Ask empowering questions such as:

What do I need to do now to get my end result?

What boundaries do I need to set?

When does it have to be done by?

What could the challenges be?

How will I overcome those challenges?

Chapter 6.
Hustle and Flow Goal Setting

The concept of Hustle and Flow is seen in many different books, events, and coaching forums; however, they mostly seem to teach these concepts in isolation of the other.

You can have a great ACTION PLAN, but without accompanying that with your Energy Plan — your results are limited and so will be your success.

This stuff is a game changer and can take your ability to manifest to the next level. This last section of the book we pull it all together! You will see how to use both aspects of your Hustle and Flow and apply it to goal setting. Many reasons why we are not as successful as we want to be getting results are because we may be missing one of these key five elements. So keep these points in mind as you read through this chapter.

Ground Rules for Effectively Setting and Achieving Your Goals

As you read the formula below, notice the following:

1. Notice what steps you already do great — high five yourself and keep doing that!

2. Notice what you rarely do, or start and stop doing. Pay attention to this and incorporate THIS into your goal setting consistently.

3. Notice the area you hate doing most — THIS is your golden nugget. Pay the most attention to that area!!!

4. Lastly, remember the power is in the combination of Action Plan and Energy Plan — so no cherry-picking just the areas you are comfortable with doing!

Let's Begin!!!

Hustle, Flow, Flow, Hustle — Hustle/Flow

Imagine you are teaching someone to dance and you are calling out the movements ...

Step — slide — slide — step — and dip!

This goal setting and achieving energy dance is just the same, only this dance is:

Hustle, Flow, Flow, Hustle — Hustle/Flow

There are Five Steps to creating and achieving truly inspiring goals that incorporate BOTH Hustle and Flow:

Step 1 —   **Hustle**: Define WHAT You Want.

Step 2 —   **Flow**: Define What You Want To FEEL.

Step 3 —   **Flow**: The Energy Plan — Align Your Vibration and Inspired Action.

Step 4 —   **Hustle**: The Action Plan —   Focus, Act, Measure.

Step 5 —   **Hustle AND Flow** — Gratitude for what is and What is Coming.

This Five Step Formula was a result of me studying how we — both my clients and I — achieved the best and quickest results. I have had a few amazing experiences where I have used this to create — and initially, it was not done consciously. But after reviewing my patterns, I also uncovered that these were the common steps I see in others who are powerful creators.

Now you may have heard some of these steps before — yet not all combined together like this!

So my Hustle peeps yes, you get to schedule and take massive action — YAY! And for my energy peeps, you get to focus on using your emotions like rocket fuel to vibrate into alignment! YAY!

Although I had been to many events (from the top of the Himalayan mountains meditating, to walking on fire, and everything in between), read the books and watched every Oprah special on creating results in your life — truly, it never all clicked together for me as powerfully as it did when I designed the amazing results in my own life. And I have a few mind-blowing ones — you know ... when those things happen in your life. When you tell the story to someone it usually starts with "You will NEVER believe what just happen to me," said usually with eyes wide open and jazz hands (go ahead picture that ... you know what I mean right?). Yes, those results.

So, here's a back-story to keep you up to speed...

I had been working for a company for many years, right out of university. I stayed there, although I never really loved the job. I had lots of beliefs about how money was made, what a "good" job was. I linked a "steady job with security" and considered people who went after their entrepreneurial dreams as wild and risky. I was also the breadwinner at the time as my husband just coming out of the army after over 10 ten years service. My job paid the bills for our house, two cars and all the other "stuff that you are supposed to have," while he was in this transition. We had two babies and well ... I felt I HAD NO CHOICE but to keep working there.

I linked this job to security and convinced myself somehow that I had to stay there for the betterment of my family (insert my eye roll right about here!).

The metaphor for my job was the golden handcuffs — I had tons of benefits, years of service, and right on the tipping point of security with a sweet pension that would give me life's sweet freedom at fifty-five. I was promoted up the chain — mostly the only female in the room, youngest, and often the leader. My life was all mapped out for me — until one day everything changed and I made a new decision.

You see, I had moved close to my parents so they could watch my kids while I went to work. That worked out great, even though I was missing a lot of my first child's time. And the work was taking its toll on me.

Then I got pregnant with my daughter. When I returned to work (60-hour weeks were normal and totally full of stress), I knew I wanted a different experience. But I had no idea HOW. It seemed impossible financially.

Then one day it all changed ... my father had a heart attack.

My parents were moving out of the city so he could recover. That meant my kids would go to daycare, which would be okay for my son, but my daughter was very fragile and sensitive. I knew she would not thrive at a daycare and to be honest, I didn't want her to go. I have no judgment on daycare — I just knew in my heart is was not a fit for her at that time.

So that day I made a DECISION and got CLEAR on what I wanted (even though I had NO IDEA HOW this would be possible).

I wanted to leave my job and I wanted them to give me a severance package to do so. Now here is the thing, my company was NOT letting people go at the time. Actually, they had approached me about taking my boss' job. So yes, that's right, I was supposed to take promotion and instead, I was looking for a way out!

I knew that I needed to make this happen before my parents moved (time bound). I knew how much money I needed (this is the first step of the action plan clarity on what you want with specific measurable and time sensitive).

The second thing I did is that I connected so very strongly to my WHY — I had a massive emotional response to it. And, I was SO clear on my WHY and so emotionally charged in the direction of my goal, I believed it would happen because I would except nothing less.

I used my emotions to fuel my drive. I envisioned and vibrationally-aligned with my end goal.

Every day (sometimes many times a day!), I connected to the end goal as if it had already happened and I was grateful for it. I had no doubt it would happen.

Even though, honestly, the world around me never gave clues it was possible.

If I had looked to the external world only for feedback, I would have given up on my dream ...

And, because I was so aligned with my end goal, I could receive inspirations, ideas (hunches as Napoleon Hill calls it), and my intuition to guide my next steps. It kept my mindset sharp to see opportunities ... and they came!

So let's hit pause here —

Consider something you made happen that once seemed like an impossible goal? Was it getting your house? Your mate? A job? Traveling? What amazing goal did you make happen that, at the time you desired it — seemed impossible and you had NO IDEA how you would make it happen?

Write down what that goal was — even if it sounded ridiculous at the time:

What did you ultimately make happen?

How clear were you about the details/vision of this goal?

What was the strong emotional reason why you wanted it?

Did you "dream" or spend time thinking and envisioning this goal in an emotionally-charged way often?

Did you have a straight outlined action plan and did you note a few unexpected hints, synchronicities or "interesting things" happening along the way to guide or assist you? If so, what 'coincidences' or 'happy accidents' occurred?

Did you take action when you needed to?

Where you grateful for the result when it happened — and how did you express that gratitude.

Hmmm. Interesting. right? See, to some extent, you have just described how you used some or all parts of this Five Step Formula to create the above goal.

Let's keep going here, as unraveling of the Five Step Formula has begun! What is interesting to note, is that usually for our most amazing dreams, the big scary ones we want so bad — well, at the start, we have NO IDEA how this can happen.

At the beginning all you know (and all you need to know) is WHAT you want. And this brings us to Step 1.

Step 1 HUSTLE: Clarity on the Goal and/or Impact You Want to Make

Yes, I appreciate this may sound basic or goal setting 101 here — but this first phase often determines your overall success.

Consider your ability to define your goal similar to that of getting GPS co-ordinates ... you can either be general in your directions for your goal (and spend a lot of time driving around the blocks, slowing the car down, and having to ask for more specific directions as you go), OR you can nail down the specific address of your target — make the journey shorter and more fun.

Now, in my experience this can often be the most challenging part for people for a few reasons.

Most people know more about what they DO NOT WANT then what they DO want.

People tend to focus on the HOW at this point and it limits them from getting a goal/impact they are really excited about. DO NOT figure out HOW you will get the goal that this point — just figure out WHAT you want. Not only will we get to the HOW — we will define both an energy plan and action plan for it!

For people who resonate with Hustle energy more so, this step may be easier. Defining the details, making a decision, and slapping a time on it, are part of how they show up.

For people who may focus more on the Flow side and energy aspect, this part is not as easy. As discussed in Chapter 5, it has nothing to do with ability — more to do with wanting to take into account all options, impacts, and feelings that come with making a decision (which can feel final).

When you can get better at defining your goal with clarity, this really is a game changer — especially for my highly energetic beings!

Consider this action to be the container to laser focus that amazing energy, rocket-fuel-charged emotion, and intention.

We are going to talk more about this in the next step below. All this is great, but without a direct focus for it, well, it is like those hand held sparklers. You know the ones that are beautiful, wild and unpredictable, and you hold them as they spew fiery sparkles everywhere!

Now, instead, consider the larger firework that is directed up at the sky, with timing, precision, and a nice big BOOM just for effect.

Well ... that is what happens when you are able to get your Goal defined. It is like designing the perfect container to send your rock of desire through to achieve maximum results.

Anything we want is primarily because of how it will make us — and the other people involved — feel.

Now, I know this is a HUSTLE step, but the FLOW of the feeling you will get from accomplishing your goal is one of the driving forces, so here are a few questions to ask yourself when defining your goal:

What do I want?

This needs to be specific and measurable. For instance, "more money" is not specific. You could instead say something like, "an additional $10,000 per month from my new business", or "to lose 2 pounds per week, every week, for the next ten weeks."

When do I want it?

Set specific dates — and remember to put a month and year on them. None of this cheating and saying, "well, it just said by the beginning of the year — it didn't say which year!"

What do I want to feel when I get it?

Go deep on this — honestly, how will you FEEL when you are making that extra $10k/month or when you have lost that 20 pounds?

If I don't get off my butt and do this NOW, what will it cost me?

Answer this one, not just in dollar terms of what it may cost you, but also Flow terms of the cost emotionally.

Often I experience people having a challenge defining at a detailed level what they want. Many people think they know what they want — but when you really dig down to the details, you realize you just have a general idea. Sometimes it is related to fears that come with setting a goal — the work that comes with it, the fear of it not coming true, etc. This is where working with someone like a mentor or coach can really help by flushing this out, getting clarity, and overcoming any beliefs holding you back from setting the goal.

For now, if you are still having issues getting clarity and making a decision on your goal, answer the following questions:

What impact is my procrastination or indecision having on my family? My relationships? My job? My Finances?

What information do I need to help me make a decision and get clarity on this goal?

So, before we go further — make sure you have a goal to work with here and test this formula out!

Write down your goal and make sure it is specific, has a date on it for when you want the goal to be achieved, and it is measurable.

My Goal, WHEN I will achieve it and WHY I want to:

You need to be able to check back in and see if you are moving towards or away from your goal. This will help you adjust your action and energy plans!

Having a vague idea of what you want isn't enough — You need to know what you want, when you want it and why you want it!

Step 2 FLOW: The Energy Plan — The Feelings and the Why

Right. Now that we have your goal defined and we have touched on why it's important — now, it's time to dial- in your energy toward it.

This where we take your clearly defined goal and inject it with steroids (really healthy, organic, energetic steroids).

Remember the question from our first step — what do you want to feel? Well, you use that answer in two ways:

1) To make sure WHAT you want (the goal you defined), is going to get you the feelings you are after. For example, if you said you wanted three million dollars, then next question is how do you want to feel? The answer may surprise you. Because you may not want the three million just to hide that under your mattress.

You may want that three million dollars to feel financial freedom, the ability to pay off your mortgage and feel that you have a beautiful space for your family to live that you own. You may want to feel like you have the freedom to quit a job you do not love and start a company you do love!

You may want to feel you can provide opportunities for your family to learn and experience via travel.

There can be a lot of FEELINGS that come with WHY you want this goal.

You want to use this feeling like rocket fuel.

From my personal and professional experience, it is not necessarily the people with the best plan that get a goal, it's the people who are most connected to WHY they want the goal. These are the people who stay hungry for it and do not give up!

2) To use it for your energy plan! Your emotions help guide you to line up your vibration. You use them to create and visualize with feeling your end goal, and it helps you in the area of feeling gratitude. These FEELINGS are a big deal — so Hustle peeps listen up here!

If you are not fully using your feelings, you are capping your results.

Flow peeps — you know this is the real deal ... but do you know HOW to use the feelings to make you more success-ful?

Keep reading!

What Is Vibration?

You may have heard this word before — for those of you who are used to getting "into their vortex" (a little Abraham Hicks* energy reference for my Flow peeps), you will know this content. But whether this is familiar territory or not, it will be good for a quick review.

I will honestly say this is the one area that made the biggest impact in my ability to create.

So what is vibration? Great question!

According to Wikipedia, vibration is defined as: an electromagnetic wave.*

... a person's emotional state (this is why your feelings are so important in the creation process), the atmosphere of a place (for example so places have a different feeling then others), or the associations of an object, as communicated to and felt by others.*

To be clear — vibration is not a feeling.

Vibration, as mentioned is an electromagnetic wave that we interpret into feelings, sounds, things we see, etc. We are all day, every day, interpreting vibrations. Now, we can go down the rabbit hole pretty deep on this topic.

On my website (*www.LisaToste.com*) I list some amazing resources you can read, watch, or listen to on this topic. And

:ely suggest you do, as this is a topic that changed how I view being able to create anything I want in my life.

For the sake of being concise on how to use vibration to create your goal (and to avoid adding on another hundred pages to this book), I will summarize this by saying this:

How we __FEEL__ is the perfect indicator as to whether we are on our path or not — whether the goal is truly something we want with heart-felt passion, or just something we just think we want ...

What Is The Law of Attraction?

The Law of Attraction says that which is like unto itself, is drawn.*

In other words, that which you think, in any moment, attracts unto itself other thoughts that are like it. That is why whenever you are thinking about a subject that is not pleasant, in a very short period of time, most of you, upon any subject that you ponder very long, attract enough supporting data that it does bring forth the essence of the subject of the thought into your experience.

Many people get caught up in the whole law of attraction thing and say, "well, I'm thinking about having more money and I clearly don't have more money!"

Actually, ever subject is two subjects — the presence of it and the absence of it.

For instance, you say you are thinking about more money — but isn't the truth that you want more money because you are thinking about the fact that you don't have enough?

I know it's hard to think about the opposite of what's right in front of you, but that's what you need to do if you are to nail this part of the formula.

You need to believe so strongly in the 'feeling' of achieving your goal, that it doesn't matter what 'reality' tells you!

Step 3 FLOW: The Energy Plan — Vibration and Inspired Ideas

Before planning, get into the vibrational alignment or mindset or state of your end goal. Meaning, before you do your planning, scheduling, or taking actions, you want to ensure that you are operating from a space vibrationally aligned with your end goal.

You want to be able to tap into a consciousness that is larger than our limited minds, which are based on our current experiences and beliefs.

Think of it this way, for someone who has only ever made $50,000 a year — taking the steps to make $150,000 may be challenging to figure out. This is when you need to take on the energy, beliefs, and mindset of someone who makes $150,000 to even understand how to get started.

Sounds good, but how do you do that, right? Well, this is where mentors, coaches, and people who have done these activities can help you break out of your limiting beliefs, shift your focus, and your energy.

Consider creating a dream-board of your goal, where you cut out pictures of what your goal looks and feels like ...

Consider taking time to meditate on your goal ...

Consider doing a visualization exercise where you imagine your goal so vividly, it feels like it has already come to pass.

VISUALIZE that you have already achieved your goal! You need to vibrationally become the person who has the goal before the goal will show up.

Have you ever heard the analogy 'dress for the job you want?' Well, the clothes have nothing to do with it. Your mindset, how you feel about yourself, and the confidence you get to take actions are impacted by how you *feel* you look.

When you vibrationally become the person who has the goal, you discover a flood of messages from your inner guidance, inspired actions from your intuition — not just the type of actions that come from our limited consciousness or thinking, but the "I just had a crazy idea to do this ..." That "out of the blue" inspiration to go talk to someone, go get a specific new book ... that leads to something amazing in line with your goal that you never could have foreseen.

Think about the way sportspeople train today — a significant part of their training is visualization.*

If it's part of the regime for elite sportspeople — a discipline where 'actual' as opposed to 'mental' work would seem most beneficial, then it's good enough for me!

Step 4 HUSTLE: The Action Plan — Plan, Take Action, Measure, REPEAT!

Now that you have clarity on the goal you want, you know how to use your feelings (your why for this goal) as rocket fuel, and you know how to use your vibration to align you with inspired actions — you are ready to start your Hustle Action Plan.

As Martin Luther King said, "You don't have to see the whole staircase, just take the first step." *

Or, as Jack Canfield* (of 'Chicken Soup for the Soul' fame) regularly mentions, that you can drive at night for miles and miles and miles — and at any time you can only see a few hundred feet in front of you — yet, you keep driving ...*

You don't need to know every step to achieve your goal, you just need to know the first few ...

Key steps of for your action plan are:

1. **Outline what actions** you need to take in order to achieve your goal

2. **Assign a duration of time to them and SCHE-DULE IT!** Yes, on a calendar — and if you can make it pop up on your phone, all the better. If you don't schedule your time, trust me someone else will do it for you — and I can guarantee they won't be getting you to do actions to achieve YOUR goals, they will be actions to achieve THEIRS!

3. **Ask yourself what resources** (people, training, books) will help you take the actions you need. Find out what these are and also schedule time to make these items happen!

4. **Measure** — yes you've got to do this! Check in frequently (and how often depends on how the timing of your goal). If you don't have a mentor or coach, I find the best way to do this is asking yourself focused questions:

Ask yourself — Am I moving closer to my goal?

Am I moving fast enough to reach my goal date?

Where do I feel resistance or where am I stuck?

To achieve your goal, you don't need to know every step from beginning to end. Simply PLAN the first few steps, take INSPIRED AC-TION, MEASURE the results — and REPEAT!

Step 5 Hustle AND Flow: Gratitude for What Is and What is Coming

Whether you are operating predominantly from a position of Hustle or Flow, gratitude is extremely important — and not necessarily in the ways you may think.

Research presented by the University of Massachusetts Dartmouth, suggests that not only does maintaining a state of gratitude potentially lower the risks of coronary disease, but also "higher reported levels of alertness, enthusiasm, determination, attentiveness, energy, and sleep duration and quality."*

I don't know about you, but if being in a state of gratitude results in having higher levels of those attributes, count me in!

*"Train yourself never to put off the word or action for the expression of gratitude." Albert Schweitzer**

We all know there is a relationship between what we think and how we feel. Part of the Hustle/Flow process is using gratitude to enhance our feelings of wellbeing in the 'now' to make us more receptive to the (FLOW), inner voice, and intuition, guiding us to inspired actions and give us more (HUSTLE) of the alertness and determination required to follow through.

The trick with gratitude in the Hustle-Flow goal setting and achieving process is being grateful for what is as well as what is coming — even before it gets here!

Putting It All Together!

Remember when the book opened with the analogy of the "Energy-Infused, Action-Plan Martini?

Recipe includes equal amounts of masculine and feminine energy, a few shots of quantum physics, a dash of intuition, a sprinkle of vortex talk, large doses of massive action, and beautifully garnished with a decorative umbrella of gratitude.

That's what we have covered in this book — a completely new way to achieve your goals, taking into account both your Hustle and your Flow.

Does the world really need another goal setting strategy?

Uhm, YES it does — well, to be more accurate this is a complete strategy that combines the best of both the Hustle and the Flow! So, it is not entirely a new strategy; it is more of one which includes the best of all approaches and combines them into one overall goal setting process.

It's the power of logical thinking and the force of heart-centred energy.

I have used this strategy in my life, with my clients, and with companies I have coached. This process helps you create the incredible type of results where YOU start a conversation with, "You will NOT believe what I just made happen!"

Truly — this is the ultimate way to achieve the results and create the impact you want. I am absolutely passionate about helping you become successful. *And to be clear, I mean success on your own terms, whatever that means*. Sometimes it is helping a company achieve the Big B (Billion-dollar) threshold — other times it is helping an overwhelmed mom find some consistent "me time."

I truly believe we design our experiences and we have power beyond what we may be comfortable to admit ... achieving a goal or creating an impact is so much more than just the THING or stuff that is created. It is about becoming the most powerful versions of ourselves in the process — using all the gifts and resources that are available to us. The logical, the illogical, the scheduled, and the inspired actions ... all of it. It's taking both camps (the masculine Hustle and the feminine Flow) and joining them together for one big bang creation!

IF you really think about it ... isn't all creation started by combining both the essence of masculine and feminine?

Hmmm ... right? Think about it!

Lisa Toste

References*

Over the years I have been influenced by the great work of many people on this topic who have helped me form my ideas, knowledge, and approach to this topic. I want to do my best highlight those resources ... while many are saying similar pieces of information, I felt it honourable to give them all credit. Some I have been able to reference with a web link or similar, others I simply honor with a notation that my work is in part a reality because of their contribution to our world. *Thank you.*

http://www.thegrindstone.com/2011/05/31/career-management/study-women-will-succeed-in-the-workplace-more-if-they-monitor-how-masculine-they-come-off/#ixzz3wPdw84gC

http://goodmenproject.com/featured-content/5-steps-to-craft-a-company-culture-with-gender-energy-balance-dsh/

http://www.thefemininewoman.com/2010/04/are-you-masculine-feminine-or-neutral-a-quiz/

http://www.gotoquiz.com/feminine_masculine_energy_quiz

http://www.forbes.com/sites/womensmedia/2012/05/07/a-balance-of-both-masculine-and-feminine-strengths-the-bottom-line-benefit/

Speech by Mark Logue on Masculine & Feminine Energy Oct 2015 AST Training.

http://lonerwolf.com/the-anima-and-animus/

The Althea Doctrine

The Queen's Code

Ask and it is Given

Into the Vortex

AST Training Provided in July 2013

http://www.huffingtonpost.com/2013/11/20/divorce-causes-_n_4304466.html

https://masteringalchemy.com/content/truth-about-masculine-and-feminine-energy-part-one

https://masteringalchemy.com/content/truth-about-masculine-and-feminine-energy-part-one

http://www.mikestaver.com/updates/communicating-with-the-opposite-gender/

http://www.forbes.com/sites/womensmedia/2012/05/07/a-balance-of-both-masculine-and-feminine-strengths-the-bottom-line-benefit/

http://knowledge.wharton.upenn.edu/article/the-masculine-and-feminine-sides-of-leadership-and-culture-perception-vs-reality/

http://kdmcmillan.com/your-leadership-style-more-feminine-or-masculine/

https://books.google.ca/books?id=-I6JW52pVzQC&pg=PA75&lpg=PA75&dq=leadership+feminine+and+masculine+energy+styles&source=bl&ots=T6PsP0GLwV&sig=cq0l3X5i3eewd5_bzOnmrYllB9Y&hl=en&sa=X&ved=0CDkQ6AEwCGoVChMI7uHVjY6zyAIVB5ENCh3l6wQo#v=onepage&q=leadership%20feminine%20and%20masculine%20energy%20styles&f=falsehttp://goodmenproject.com/featured-content/5-steps-to-craft-a-company-culture-with-gender-energy-balance-dsh/

http://www.jamesgrayrobinson.com/news/2015/7/24/balancing-masculine-and-feminine-energies-at-works

http://lonerwolf.com/the-anima-and-animus/

http://www.thefemininewoman.com/2010/04/are-you-masculine-feminine-or-neutral-a-quiz/

http://www.gotoquiz.com/feminine_masculine_energy_quiz

Acknowledgements

Without the help of many people, I could not have completed this book.

First thank you to my children who inspire me to be a better person each day. To my husband who, as you have read, walks a journey with me where we are constantly learning and playing with this topic of hustle and flow.

To my dear friends Dianne, Colette, Brenda, and my mother-in-law Patricia, who were always cheering me on to keep going!

To my dear friend Chris, who walked the path before me and connected me with the fabulous Leigh. Thanks to her efforts, encouragement, skill, and lots of patience, this book has become all I had hoped it would be in order to help others create their own personal success.

Lastly to a dear friend and leader , who kept the pressure on to live my purpose.

To all above, I thank you, I love, and I am forever grateful for you being in my life.

About Lisa Toste

Lisa is a mother of two fabulous children and has been with her husband Alex for over thirteen years, and still counting! She is a consumer of adventure and fun — while at the same time, also being very focused on intentionally creating her life and leaving a positive impact on the world.

She is passionate about people creating their own personal versions of success and feeling empowered to turn that into reality!

She is world traveler, visiting over twenty countries, with plans to continue to explore many more! She has travelled to the tops of the Himalayan peaks in Nepal and spent a month learning from Tibetan monks (big time Flow Energy) — to the other extreme of professional speaking and coaching companies and successful entrepreneurs all over the world (big time Hustle Energy), on creating results.

Her interest for personal development started in university while completing her Psychology degree and continued into her corporate years.

After many years, she left her "safe and secure" job to start her own business and live life on her own terms as a woman, a mother, and a wife. Now she helps women, men, and companies define their versions of success (personally and professionally), and set up the action plan and the energy plan to make it happen!

Lisa can best be described as strong, intuitive, focused on results, driven to create a massive impact on the world, and overall, a person who is *in love with life!*

For more information, and your 'thank you for reading this book' invitation to join Lisa Toste on a special LIVE webinar where YOU get to ask the questions that are most pressing in your world, please visit:

www.LisaToste.com.

1225 Duff Dr.

Mtn + Riverside
Ft. Collins
Conoco Gas

309 - 3370
382

482 - 0159
Choice Town
Dona

Made in the USA
San Bernardino, CA
11 January 2019